THE FORBIDDEN KNOWLEDGE OF
The Book of Enoch

THE FORBIDDEN KNOWLEDGE OF
𝔗𝔥𝔢 𝔅𝔬𝔬𝔨 𝔬𝔣 𝔈𝔫𝔬𝔠𝔥

The Watchers, Nephilim,
Fallen Angels, and the
End of the World

HAROLD ROTH

WEISER BOOKS

This edition first published in 2024 by Weiser Books, an imprint of

Red Wheel/Weiser, LLC
With offices at:
65 Parker Street, Suite 7
Newburyport, MA 01950
www.redwheelweiser.com

Copyright © 2024 by Harold Roth

All rights reserved. No part of this publication may be reproduced or transmitted in any form or by any means, electronic or mechanical, including photocopying, recording, or by any information storage and retrieval system, nor used in any manner for purposes of training artificial intelligence (AI) technologies to generate text or imagery, including technologies that are capable of generating works in the same style or genre, without permission in writing from Red Wheel/Weiser, LLC. Reviewers may quote brief passages.

ISBN: 978-1-57863-812-3

Library of Congress Cataloging-in-Publication Data available upon request.
Cover by Sky Peck Design
Interior by Debby Dutton
Typeset in Adobe Garamond Pro and Frutiger LT Standard

Printed in the United States of America
IBI
10 9 8 7 6 5 4 3 2 1

For the seekers

Contents

Acknowledgments		ix
Introduction		xi

Part One: The History of Enoch 1

Chapter 1	The History of The Book of Enoch	3
Chapter 2	Jewish History and Apocalyptic Works	17
Chapter 3	Giants, Demons, and Babylon	29
Chapter 4	Magic and Enoch at Qumran	41
Chapter 5	Enoch and the Canon in Judaism	49
Chapter 6	Enoch in Early Christianity	55
Chapter 7	The Evolution of the Watchers	63
Chapter 8	The Astronomical Book	79

Part Two: Characters in Enoch 87

Chapter 9	Enoch: Man and Something More	89
Chapter 10	The Watchers: Angels and Something Less	93
Chapter 11	The Wives	107

Chapter 12	The Nephilim	117
Chapter 13	Noah	121
Chapter 14	The Righteous	125
Chapter 15	The Babylonian Exorcists	133
Chapter 16	Christian Responses to the Watchers' Teachings: Women Are Evil	143

Part Three: Other Enochic Works   151

Chapter 17	The Book of Jubilees	153
Chapter 18	The Rape of Dinah	161
Chapter 19	The Book of Giants	165
Chapter 20	Other Books of Enoch	169
Chapter 21	Enoch in Occulture	175

Conclusion	179
Appendix: Timeline of The Book of Enoch	187
Glossary	189
Notes	191
Bibliography	199

Acknowledgments

I'd like to thank my excellent editors, Judika Illes and Rachel Nagengast, without whose editorial work and active listening this text would not exist.

Introduction

And Enoch walked with God, and he was no longer,
for God had taken him.

—Genesis 5:24

More than two thousand years after it was written, The Book of Enoch continues to draw readers. Part of its attraction is its hiddenness, a kind of secrecy that has been the source of various conspiracies about why it was not available for centuries in the West. Part of the problem was that almost no religious practice adopted it into the company of their approved sacred texts—the canon, whether that is the Hebrew Bible or Christian scripture (for the most part). Because of this, The Book of Enoch was basically lost (to the West) for centuries.

What's important to us now is that because of this loss, some today believe that its disappearance resulted from the book's suppression by religious powers especially those of the Christan church. The implication has been that something about The Book of Enoch's contents was considerd not fit for general consumption or that the book contained secret information that threatened the authority of Chrisitianity and Judaism. Since its rediscovery (by the West) in the 18th century, readers have sought its secrets—its forbidden knowledge. But often contemporary readers have been baffled by its contents—mostly because the general population is not acquainted with the history of the Temple of Jerusalem or the Temple priesthood. What's more, readers can be overwhelmed by the fact that the book contains a number of versions of the same events that actually contradict each other. Readers who are perhaps accustomed to approaching sacred texts as if they had a single, unified voice, will find The Book of Enoch's contadictory contents baffling and even disturbing.

However, if we look at the history of this work and its relationship to Judaism and Christianity, we discover that this book was not suppressed or forbidden by anyone at any time. It simply lost its usefulness to religious authorities in terms of representing the doctrines of those religions as they changed over time and was therefore left in the shed to rust into nothingness like any discarded tool.

An ancient text, The Book of Enoch was originally written in Aramaic, or more particularly Jewish Babylonian Aramaic, a relative of Hebrew commonly used in Jewish writings from about the time of the Jewish capitivity in Babyon (597–537 BCE) until the writing of the Talmud (up through the 11th century CE). Enoch began to be written around 300 BCE in Judea (which, since the invasion by Jordan in the 1980s, has been known as the West Bank). It was translated into a variety of other languages over the years.

The most influential section has always been The Book of the Watchers, which is the second oldest part.

In spite of its loss of utility to dogma, The Book of Enoch remains potent for many of us. It both hides and reveals its treasures, teasing and tempting with its beauty and power, much as the Church Fathers envisioned the women who learned how to beautify themselves thanks to the Watchers' gifts. But if those gifts resulted in an explosion of violence in the ancient world depicted in The Book of Enoch, they can help us to navigate our tumultuous time and perhaps get a real handle on how to practice *tikkun olam,* the manadatory work of healing of the universe, for which all of us are responsible.

The Book of Enoch springs from a kernel of a story mentioned in Genesis 6:1–8. In Genesis, several generations after the creation of the first human beings, people already fill the Earth. A group of angels, the Watchers, look down from their places and see how beautiful the daughters of human beings are. They go down to Earth and take women for their wives. The Nephilim, their children, are described as very large, with rapacious appetites of all kinds. They ate not only human beings, but each other, and they raped animals of all kinds. They killed most human beings on Earth before the Divine sent a Flood to wipe them out. Only Noah was spared.

This story is greatly expanded in the oldest part of The Book of Enoch, The Book of Watchers, which goes back to at least 300 BCE in Judea (what is now called the West Bank). But scholars believe that the stories it is based on go back even farther. Over and over, in all sorts of different cultures, we hear stories about heavenly beings coming down to Earth and interacting with human beings in some way, whether they are in the form of myths like Prometheus or Lucifer bringing fire or light to people or modern tales of aliens inspiring and helping us. Clearly the concept of an interaction between Heaven and Earth has often been important to us.

But just like any story, the tale of how the Watchers came down to Earth is developed and used for various purposes. Jewish scribes bundle The Watchers with The Astronomical Book, a work that lays out an original system of astronomy, and in turn, these are grouped with The Book of Similitudes, The Book of Dream Visions, and The Epistles of Enoch. However, regardless of the religious milieu, The Watchers is the center of interest in The Book of Enoch, and for that reason, I focus most of my book on that story and its characters.

At least two different older tales were combined in The Watchers. One held the Watcher Shemihazah (pronounced Shem-ee-kha-ZAH) at its center, and the other Asael (pronounced Ah-sah-AYL). I've used the spellings for these angels' names because that is how they are spelled by scholars who can read the Aramaic fragments of Enoch found at Qumran. Other versions of their names are often found, some based on Greek (Azazel); Slavonic (Azael); Hebrew for a different fellow's name (Azazel, who was the representation of the barren desert area that received the scapegoat

Introduction **xiii**

ritually bearing the sins of the Israelites); or other versions using Victorian transliteration systems. Likewise, the name Shemihazah is encountered for similar reasons as Samyaza, Aza, Uzza, Ouza, Shemiaza, and many more.

These two angels brought very different bodies of forbidden knowledge to human beings. Shemihazah brought traditional occult arts like divination through all sorts of natural signs, from types of lightning to astrology, and dark arts like spellwork, including cursing and pacts (which is why, later, the introduction of writing is cursed, even though Enoch is himself a scribe, and he is praised for inventing writing). Asael brings the forbidden knowledge of metalwork, focusing on making armor, swords, and spears—the instruments of war—a way of distorting and debasing metalworking, changing it from forging instruments of agriculture, like hoes, shovels, and plows, to instruments of death. But like an old-time alchemist, he also brings the forbidden knowledge of dyes, silversmithing, and cosmetics. These are used by human beings, both men and women, to entice others into illicit sex, and that comes to be seen as the greater evil of the two bodies of forbidden knowledge the Watchers bring.

The Nephilim are destroyed by the Flood, but due to a variety of circumstances, scraps of the Nephilim are allowed to survive to bedevil humans in the future, and what's more, the forbidden knowledge still lives—mostly through writing.

We also see with the history of The Book of Enoch how it originally provided an alternative explanation for how evil came to be in this world. It completely ignores the story of Adam and Eve, Cain and Abel, dislodging the origin of evil from humans and instead shifting it to Heaven, with the actions of the Watchers. Likewise, the real problem with evil, we are told, is not that humans disobeyed God or engaged in murder but that if there is any original sin, it is that the Watchers broke with divine order and abandoned their posts as guides of stars. In so doing, they let loose chaos in the sky and brought that chaos with them down to Earth and to human beings. We recall how creation was made from chaos—*tohu* and *bohu,* from which God created an orderly world, where rains came at appropriate times and we could tell the seasons by the orderly stars, moon, and sun. The order is shattered by the Watchers caving to their own desire for sex and the resulting children (both of which are meant for humans, not angels). The Watchers' own selfishness led to the destruction of the world.

Part of the forbidden knowledge of The Book of Enoch is the systems of divination, metalworking, and the alchemical arts of coloring materials. But another part of its forbidden knowledge is the alternative and hidden story of the source of evil in the world. We must conclude that at least in some way, the Divine is the ultimate source of evil, since the Watchers were divinely created and obtained the knowledge they spread to humans from Heaven. Humans involve themselves in using and spreading this knowledge, but they didn't invent it and are not the origin of it.

Further, The Book of Enoch depicts God allowing evil to exist— basically encouraging it—by permitting 10 percent of the evil spirits of the Nephilim to continue to exist after the Flood.

Another aspect of the forbidden knowledge the Watchers bring to earth is just how forbidden it was, how deformed and crooked, and where that deformation came from. We must wrestle with the idea of whether this knowledge was wrong from the beginning, that it was somehow stolen as a corrupt and corrupting product of Heaven, or if it became corrupt and corrupting by being take out of Heaven and spread among human beings by the Watchers—which, of course, implies that the angels are themselves corrupt.

The idea that angels could be corrupt—that ultimately Heaven was responsible for evil—bothered religious thinkers enough to end up rejecting The Book of Enoch as false. Both Jewish and Christian authorities had come to consider that evil came to be on Earth strictly through human activity, such as disobeying God's commandment that they must not eat from the fruit of the Tree of the Knowledge of Good and Evil or murder their own brother out of jealousy (Cain and Abel).

There are two other types of forbidden knowledge in The Book of Enoch. One is the framing of The Book of Enoch as a critique of the corruption of the priests of the Temple of Jerusalem once they returned from Babylonian exile, bringing a lot of Babylonian corruption like their lunar calendar, which messed up the timetable of festivals, and various occult practices of the Babylonian exorcists, especially divination and root-cutting. These practices could be seen as corrupt and corrupting in their origin, coming from the hated Babylonian conquerors. But this forbidden knowledge could also be seen as corrupt from the perspective that it simply was not effective, according to Enoch.

The other forbidden knowledge that might be part of the critique that is The Book of Enoch is the fact that when the former priests of the Temple of Jerusalem returned from exile, they brought not only divination and spellwork but also foreign wives, and they did not abide by accepted laws of ritual purity with respect to their relationship with women. Marriage as corrupt and corrupting is important in The Book of Enoch, but it was also very important in the non-priestly critique of the Temple priests.

Clearly, The Book of Enoch is shot through with all sorts of forbidden knowledge from which we can learn. Whether that forbidden knowledge might be harmful to us is something only we can judge. In this book, I discuss this forbidden knowledge and hope that discussion helps you to untangle the thread of what is evil, how it came to be, how it continues, and how we can involve ourselves in stopping it.

PART ONE

The History of Enoch

You will often find The Book of Enoch in collections of pseudepigrapha. Pseudepigrapha are books that claim to be written by a Biblical figure and often at an ancient period of history but were actually composed by someone else at a later point in time. They are usually written in the style of the Hebrew Bible or Christian Scriptures. They typically are not included in canonical bibles. Examples include The Book of Noah, Apocalypse of Adam, Testament of Solomon, or The Book of Enoch. Why would anyone write a book and claim it was written by someone else, especially a figure from ancient times, when these "authors" describe seeing visions of Heaven, prophesize, or transmit revelations they say were inspired by interaction with the Divine? Doesn't that seem a little bit presumptuous, maybe even blasphemous? Why would anyone claim a book was written by a saintly ancient when they wrote it themselves?

Often these books are mentioned in sacred texts that have become selectively canonical. Canonical books are those which the authorities of a religion consider to be authentically divinely inspired. They are included in the religion's main sacred text, such as the Hebrew Bible. So, for instance, The Book of Jubilees is canonical in the Catholic Church, but Enoch is canonical only in the Ethiopic Church, not in the Catholic Church, the Orthodox Church, or in Judaism, where it originated.

People working with sacred texts in the past (for instance, scribes copying books that became canonical) might look back and notice great gaps in the transmission of sacred knowledge. Consider scribes copying Genesis who question what Noah had to say about the world and his interactions with God. What were the world and the events of the Flood like from his perspective? Constructing a book that speaks for Noah helps to fill in the gaps in sacred history—which is not at all the same as secular history. When we look at the Hebrew Bible, we should keep in mind that it is not a history book. It's a sacred text that reveals some divinely inspired truths, not facts. At least, that is the approach that all but the most literal readings of a sacred text will take, and it is the approach that I will take here.

CHAPTER ONE

The History of
The Book of Enoch

When we read The Book of Enoch, we don't think that yes, angels came down to earth and had sex with human women and the result was a race of demonic critters who tried to eat up the world. We don't take that as fact, but we can take it as a truth—something with an important meaning for many of us. What The Book of Enoch talks about is as important as any fact because it is concerned with the rise of evil in the world. The bottom line is that it is not important whether the Watchers, a band of angels, "really" landed on Mount Hermon in what would become the Land of Israel to start their assault on the world. What's important is what that story means for the people who wrote that book and for us now. In the end, it does not even matter if the Watchers were "real." It matters what they *mean*.

This is, for me, tied to the issue of pseudepigrapha. To reject a book as false on the basis that it claims that it was written by one of the ancients is, to me, the equivalent of rejecting spirituality because there are no "facts" about the divine—the divine has no weight or measurement, no temperature or color. Spirituality is not a science, and science is not truth. It's fact. And while facts are important and help us make our way in the physical world, truth is just as important, if not more so, because it enables us to make our way in the world of community, relationships, society, nature, self, and the spiritual.

We often come across references to texts in other books. We might have no record of these texts other than these references. There might even be some quotes or entire extracts sprinkled around to help "prove" the existence of these texts. Perhaps the author of the book we are reading thought there *ought* to be such a book and just referred to it without ever having come across the actual book. They might be motivated by wanting to give a stronger sense of the existence of a chain of knowledge between the past and their present, or they might want to create more credibility for the ancestors of their people or group. On the other hand, the book might have been real and simply have become lost. Of all the pseudepigrapha out there, The Book of Enoch is probably the most well-known and one that actually existed—and continues to exist to this day.

The pseudepigrapha to which The Book of Enoch belongs is a distinctive group of books that were written in Aramaic in the fourth to the second centuries BCE.

At that time, Aramaic was the dominant language for the people of Israel, a result of the elite of Jerusalem having been exiled to Babylon, an ancient city on the Euphrates River in what is now Iraq. The people there originally spoke Akkadian, which was written with a stylus, but because it was so difficult to learn to read, it was gradually replaced with Old Aramaic, which in turn was adopted by Jewish exiles as Jewish Babylonian Aramaic. Because they came from the elite of Jerusalem, they were literate, and many became scribes who copied Babylonian sacred texts (remember, there were no printers at this time; books were reproduced by handwriting on scrolls). Some Jews remained in Babylon after the exiles returned to Jerusalem and became the core of the people who wrote the Babylonian Talmud, which is written in Jewish Babylonian Aramaic. (The Babylonian Talmud is the name of what is commonly called just "the Talmud" today. It contains the Mishna and the Babylonian Gemara, which is information from the oral teachings of the teachers of Talmudic schools in Iraq.) It was only when the Maccabean revolt occurred that Hebrew returned as the dominant language as an expression of nationalism.

The Maccabees were a group of guerilla fighters who conducted attacks on representatives of the colonial powers in Judea beginning in 167 BCE. Eventually they formed an army and captured Jerusalem in 164

BCE. They threw out the statue of Zeus and rededicated the Temple on the 25th of Kislev, which became the date of Hanukkah. The success of the Maccabean Revolt caused a resurgence of Jewish nationalism.

You might well imagine how important it would be for a people whose actual history is fractured by the periodic exile of chunks of its population that some sense of continuity and connection be imposed upon its past, even though Jews were continuously present in the Land of Israel over the course of thousands of years and into the present day. These pseudepigrapha describe traditions being passed down to the "present" in writing before Moses presented the Law to the Israelites at Mount Sinai. In a world that was becoming more centered on written text rather than on oral transmission of text, the fact that these traditions were written down gave them a credibility that they did not attain if they had been passed down orally. Oral knowledge had come to be less powerful or respected than written knowledge. This makes sense especially when you think about the importance of the word in Judaism; the word created a universe. These writings could explain how people who lived centuries before the revelation at Sinai still knew about certain laws that only came into existence thousands of years later.

If we focus on the story of the Watchers, the center of The Book of Enoch, we can wonder if that tale might have been passed down orally before it was ever written down. Maybe. The thing is that we don't know. We have no evidence that it was or that it wasn't. There are just too many gaps in the history.

Oral history gets ignored in societies that prize the written word. In fact, it wasn't until a few hundred years after the Temple of Jerusalem was destroyed by the occupying Romans that the idea that there was a whole body of knowledge passed down orally in Judaism, as a kind of partner to the written tradition, came to be considered important.

There have been two Temples of Jerusalem. The first was built by King Solomon in the 10th century BCE. This was destroyed by the Babylonians in 587 BCE. It was rebuilt as the Second Temple in 538 BCE and refurbished centuries later by Herod the Great. It was destroyed by the Romans in 70 CE. Seven centuries later, when the Muslims invaded and conquered Jerusalem, they built a mosque on top of the ruins. Archeological evidence of the First and Second Temple has since been found. The Temple of Jerusalem was the center of the sacrificial cult in Judaism, and was one of the places where animals, grain, or incense was sacrificed for the redemption of sins. It was and is considered the most sacred site in Judaism.

The Pharisees, who became part of the survival of Judaism after the sacrificial cult could no longer operate following the destruction of the Temple, put forward the idea of an oral tradition of the Torah, the ultimate story of the relationship between the Israelites and the Divine. The Pharisees were a group of people who came together during the Second Temple period. They opposed the Hellenism of the Sadducees, a more elite group aligned with the Temple priesthood; the Pharisees were more middle class and not part of the Temple powers that be. They believed that Mosaic law was more important than the sacrificial cult, that oral teachings were part of the Torah, and that the dead would be resurrected one day. When the elite of the Temple were exiled to Babylon, the Pharisees began conducting study houses where anyone could learn the Law rather than engaging in the sacrificial cult. Their practices became the foundation of Judaism. Since the Pharisees were basically undermining what had been a very dominating and closed power system and allowing anyone to participate in the study of sacred texts, I am not sure why Jesus felt the need to malign the Pharisees.

The Torah

The Torah is composed of the first five books of the Hebrew Bible: Genesis, Exodus, Leviticus, Numbers, and Deuteronomy. Genesis is the oldest and is thought to go back to 1900 BCE. Multiple versions of various stories are repeated with different plot turns, showing that the Torah was composed of various versions. There was no one single correct version. It contains multiple voices. Although it's fashionable in some circles to view any religion as a monolith, with only one voice and one version of truth, the fact is that religions are always as fractured as any other human-built system. This is very clearly the case in Judaism.

Even before the destruction of the Temple, the Pharisees were building study houses where anyone could come and study the sacred texts without having to pay to make sacrifices at the Temple or support a hereditary, closed priesthood that was often seen as corrupt and a failure, disconnected from the masses of Israelites and preoccupied with persnickety rules. But at the same time, the movements around the Temple priesthood, the Sadducees[1] and Zadokites,[2] rejected any idea of an oral Torah separate from the written Torah or a secretly transmitted, esoteric oral revelation. Their focus was on the written word. And to some extent, we can see that it was precisely the groups around the priesthood that ended up creating the pseudepigrapha as a way of connecting Moses, whose experience is central to the written Torah, all the way back to the creation of the world described in Genesis.

In those days, before the invention of printing, books couldn't exist without scribes. But these scribes themselves might well have developed a resentment towards the priesthood that in turn could have resulted in the creation of texts like The Book of Enoch, which some argue contain a lot of criticism of the corruption of the Temple priesthood.

Really, the only oral tradition that's mentioned in most pseudepigrapha is angels speaking to humans. But that immediately brings up an issue that will be important in The Book of Enoch and how people reacted to and interpreted it: Hebrew prophets learn revealed secrets, but they don't do it through tools like omens and signs. Instead, they learn them either directly from the Divine or from God's messengers, the angels. In other words—or *in* words—they are told. This is the reason why according to Jewish law (*Halakhah*) it's okay for Enoch to predict the future but not for Pagan diviners to do so.

Halakhah is composed of religious laws based on the commandments in the Hebrew Bible, on oral Torah such as the Talmud, and on custom. Halakhah is flexible and has been modified over the centuries so that savage laws from ancient times have been hedged around so that they can no longer be carried out. Likewise, new laws have been made that allow for a better life for Jews today. Halakhah doesn't apply to anyone but Jews.

The History of The Book of Enoch

Divination is fine in this system if it comes through one's connection to God; the Hebrew prophets are "specialized diviners." Prophecy and divination can be combined without worrying about it being wrong—a good example of this is in the Hebrew Bible with the prophetess Huldah, who, when asked a question, doesn't throw lots or read innards; instead, she asks God, who answers her directly. This direct connection to the Divine as the engine for divination is exactly what powers various apocalyptic texts like The Book of Enoch or the Book of Daniel. Written 164 BCE, the Book of Daniel is the most recent book included in the canon of the Hebrew Bible. Written partly in Hebrew and partly in Aramaic, it focuses a good deal on dreamwork. Its main figure is a Jewish exile in Babylon who is able to interpret the king's dreams when the court dream diviners cannot do so.

Enoch's Connection to Genesis

Most discussions of how The Book of Enoch is connected to canonical Jewish or Christian sacred writings mention a couple of small sections of Genesis.

The first section is Genesis 5:18–24:

When Jared had lived 162 years, he begot Enoch.
After the birth of Enoch, Jared lived 800 years and begot sons and
    daughters.
All the days of Jared came to 962 years; then he died.
When Enoch had lived 65 years, he begot Methuselah.
After the birth of Methuselah, Enoch walked with God 300 years,
    and he begat sons and daughters.
All the days of Enoch came to 365 years.
Enoch walked with God; then he was no more, for God
    took him.

This section describes how Enoch, one of the sons of Jared, had a son, Methuselah, when he was sixty-five, when he also walked with God (Elohim). Finally, we're told that Enoch lived to be 365 years old (do you find that number significant?) and *walked with God until he was not*, because God took him. And that is pretty much everything we know about Enoch from the Hebrew Bible. We're never told that he was a prophet, that he was given revelations, that he saw the heavenly throne, that he interceded for angels who fell to Earth, or anything else. We get just a few sentences about him and then the mysterious statement about God taking him—mysterious because "God took him" has been interpreted various ways. The most important interpretations are either that Enoch simply died, or that Enoch was bodily brought up to Heaven. If the latter is true, he is the only human being who was brought bodily up to Heaven. We'll see that this bodily ascension is highly important for how The Book of Enoch is received down the years, whether it was a prized text or rejected, and how it came to serve as a proof to those who practiced heavenly ascensions as a ritual (*Hekhalot*[3] or *Merkavah*[4]) or those who sought what they perceived as foretellings of Jesus as Christ in ancient documents.

What Does Elohim Mean Anyway?

YHVH and El/Elohim are two names of the Divine in the Hebrew Bible. (The Divine has other names in that book as well.)

- El was the generic term for god in Hebrew.
- Elohim meant gods or the totality of god, supreme god, or godhead.
- YHVH (usually pronounced by simply naming the letters: Yohd Hey Vahv Hey, because the vowels are not indicated), Yahu, or Yah was the personal name of the god of Israel.

However, these two names, YHVH and El/Elohim, merged in the 15th century BCE. We can see this in the prophet Miriam's Song of the Sea (Exodus 15:20–22), "My strength and my song is Yah, and he is become my salvation, This is my god (El) and I will glorify him, the supreme god (Elohim) of my father, and I will exalt him." She sang this song to praise the Divine for saving the Israelites from the Egyptian forces by parting the Red Sea so the Israelites could cross safely and then letting the waves crash over the pursuing Egyptians, drowning them. Miriam's song was clearly a lot longer in the past, much as her role as prophet was much more extensive.

The History of The Book of Enoch

"Elohim" is a masculine plural noun.[5] It can be taken to mean "gods," "the supreme god," "angel," "spirits of the dead," or even sometimes "kings." The blurring of this category comes up particularly in The Book of Enoch in reference to the *benei ha Elohim* or "sons of (the) gods"/"sons of God." We'll see that this ambivalence becomes important for Jewish and Christian interpretations of the Watchers story and can be taken as one of the reasons why The Book of Enoch becomes lost in the West.

The Hebrew Bible is composed of at least four different accounts that were combined to make the Pentateuch (the first five books of the Hebrew Bible) that has come down to us. Each one of those accounts tends to feature a particular name of God: The name Elohim is associated with the Priestly account, which was probably written during the Babylonian Exile (608-538 BCE). This strand is the most concerned with ritual purity, the line of the priesthood extending from Aaron, genealogy, the location of shrines, the various rituals and liturgy, and other aspects that would be of particular focus for the hereditary priesthood of the Temple of Jerusalem.

There were two layers of priests in the Temple: the Zadokites, who had the privilege and responsibility of conducting the sacrifices (which would include receiving a portion of them), and the Levites, who weren't allowed to conduct sacrifices but performed other tasks and rituals. The Zadokites were the only game in town at the Temple of Jerusalem, but there were temples elsewhere in the land that had their own priests. These were left to carry on the Israelite religion after the Zadokites were taken into exile by the Babylonians when they conquered Jerusalem in 587 BCE. The Levites didn't have the power or money to carry on the sacrificial cult in the Temple of Jerusalem, and that practice fell into disarray there, but another group of priests, who styled themselves as the sons of Aaron, ran the temple in Bethel and preserved the sacrificial cult. The Zadokites wrote the Priestly source while exiled to Babylonia.

When the Babylonians lost the war with the Persian Empire in 539 BCE, the Zadokites returned from exile. They set about making the Levites subordinate again. The sons of Aaron didn't take too kindly to the Zadokites trying to renew their own power and position, but they ended up being overwhelmed; so were the Levites of Jerusalem. The Priestly source became a weapon to justify the priesthood's existence and power. Various stories were created that "proved" they deserved to control the sacrificial cult and thus claw back much power and culture in Jerusalem. This becomes an important part of Enoch, but there the Zadokites are portrayed as corrupt.

Even though Enoch's name is used in the title of The Book of Enoch, the real stars of the show are the angels, the *benei ha Elohim*. But even this group receives basically one sentence of description in Genesis—"When men began to increase on earth and daughters were born to them, the divine beings saw how beautiful the daughters of men were and took wives from among those that pleased." (Genesis 6:1) And that's it. There's nothing about these beings teaching humans anything, which is one of the most important differences in The Book of Enoch version of this event.

The next verse in the Genesis treatment of the Watchers story seems like it's going off on a tangent until we consider what it means. God describes how humans are flesh as well as God's spirit, so they will live only 120 years: "The Lord said, 'My breath shall not abide in man forever, since he also is flesh; therefore shall his days be 120 years.'" (Genesis 6:3) This does make us wonder how Enoch lived 365 years and others even longer. Why do some people live hundreds of years in the Hebrew Bible? Do they have more of God's spirit in them than the human beings who were born after them? It seems so, especially when we consider that the Flood can be viewed as a divider between two worlds on Earth, one of which is in a kind of purely mythical time, time before time began to exist, and the other which is more like historical ancient time, although it still has plenty of mythical aspects, such as some people living for hundreds of years.

Once we get to the story of the angels in The Book of Enoch, we can see that this remark about how human beings will live only 120 years serves to define the category of human beings. For one, the angels will live forever—although perhaps not, given that in The Book of Enoch version, once having left Heaven and taken wives the Watchers can no longer return to Heaven—which might well mean that God's spirit is no longer in them or has been withdrawn from them, just as it will be withdrawn from

The History of The Book of Enoch

11

humans when they hit 120. But the other importance of this seemingly unrelated remark about how long humans will live is how it stresses the difference between humans and angels. The implication, we will see, is that humans and angels should stay in their lanes. Angels live so very long and therefore have no need to have children. That means that angels marrying humans is a violation of the divine order, even though no commandment forbids intermarriage between angels and humans. In Genesis, this meaning—the violation of divine order—must be extracted; in The Book of Enoch, however, it's one of the major themes.

To me, the most difficult verse in this section is Genesis 6:4, especially when we try to connect it up to the events related in The Book of Enoch. We're told about the Nephilim: "It was then, and, later too, that the Nephilim appeared on earth—when the divine beings cohabited with the daughters of men, who bore them offspring. They were the heroes of old, the men of renown."

You'll notice that Nephilim is not translated into English, even though it's clearly a Hebrew plural noun (ending in -im). The problem is that no one is sure what the real meaning of the root of the word Nephilim means. One interpretation of the name "Nephilim" argues that it is based on the root for the verb "to fall," so we might call them the Fallen. But in fact, no one knows what the source of this word is, so most scholars nowadays just use the Hebrew word "Nephilim." I think "Nephilim" is a better choice than "Fallen," because "Fallen" is connected to the Christian story of the battle between good and bad angels in Heaven; the bad guys were kicked out and literally fell. This story does not occur in the Hebrew Bible. The Watchers of The Book of Enoch don't fall; they willingly descend to earth to take human women.

In terms of the Hebrew Bible, no connection is made between Enoch and the sons of God/the Watchers. That connection occurs only outside of the Hebrew Bible, most especially in The Book of Enoch.

Most Jews and Christians consider The Book of Enoch an outgrowth of these sections in the Hebrew Bible, but a few scholars think the situation might be just the opposite—that the Genesis sections are just a kind of footnote reference to the full story, which came before Genesis in history. Even though most people who study pseudepigrapha from this time period reject that idea, I think it's worth entertaining because it allows us to think about how different these two versions of events really are. We must wonder what those differences represent in terms of the meaning, who composed these works, what purposes they were meant to serve, and who was their intended audience.

Ezekielism

The story of the Watchers tends to be the most familiar part of The Book of Enoch. Although many later texts were influenced by that story, we don't see any similar tale coming before outside of those few lines of Genesis. But what about the rest of The Book of Enoch? Are there sections that echo what has come before in sacred texts?

Yes, and most especially Enoch's vision of Heaven and the throne of God, which relates back to such visions of the prophet Ezekiel, who saw the chariot of God (Ezekiel chapter 1). This vision in Hebrew is called Merkavah (the word for "chariot") and became the basis of an entire mystical system through which participants attempted to experience that vision personally. Although Merkavah isn't usually considered to have begun as a practice until about 100 BCE, in Merkavah writings, it is set during the Babylonian captivity, 587–538 BCE, and opens with Ezekiel sitting on the shore of a river in Babylon. He sees a cloud blown in by the north wind that carries a brilliant nimbus in which are what he calls four Cherubim— essentially Fire spirits, as all Judaic angels are. Each of these beings has four wings and four faces: one is like a man, one like a lion, one like an ox, and one like an eagle. (I have often seen these faces depicted in the corners of stained-glass windows of Christian churches as well as on the Chariot card of Rider-Waite-Smith tarot deck.) These creatures are shiny and have feet shaped like those of a calf. Two of their four wings stretch up and are joined to the wings of the others, and two cover their bodies.

The beings are described as similar to fiery coals,[6] flashes of light and of lightning, and burning torches (Ezekiel 1:13). We're told that the beings "ran and returned" (Ezekiel 1:14), which is a phrase that appears in later mystical texts, like the Sefer Yetzirah, often cited as the source of Kabbalistic ideas such as the Sephirot, representations of the emanation of the divine in the world. The prophet sees wheels next to each being. The wheels have eyes set around their rims and look like wheels within wheels. Above them was something that looks like the heavens composed of ice. Above that Ezekiel sees a sapphire[7] throne upon which sits something shaped like a man who seems to be composed of intense rainbow light, fire, and lightning. God speaks to Ezekiel and gives him a scroll to eat, which tastes like honey to the prophet.

This is the vision of the Chariot/Merkavah as the prophet Ezekiel experienced it. God also gives Ezekiel a mission to go and tell the people that if they don't heed the word of God that God will make them suffer. That's important not only for the people of Qumran, a community located south of Jericho in what is now named the West Bank, and just south of the Dead Sea, but for The Book of Enoch.

Qumran was settled by Israelites around 650 BCE. It was not a poor community of ascetics; it contained places for making fine pottery and glass that was sold in nearby Jericho, and large amounts of coins were found there. It also is famous, though, for the caves close by containing large numbers of sacred scrolls, often called the Dead Sea Scrolls. The caves were a sort of library for the community, which continued to be populated by Jews up until the Romans destroyed it.

Ezekiel's vision influences some Qumran texts, like Songs of the Sabbath Sacrifice,[8] one of their central documents and which they used to imitate what they believe occurred around the throne of the Divine. But Ezekiel is also adopted by the movement that opposed the Zadokites.

In Ezekiel's vision, the Chariot moves and takes God away from the Temple of Jerusalem; if you were a person who thought the workings of the Temple of Jerusalem were seriously flawed by issues of impurity and corruption, then that aspect of Ezekiel's vision would resonate. God has literally left the building, but we can still praise God, just as the angels around the throne do. In The Book of Enoch, the Chariot is static, but

Heaven is not; towards the end of the Book, Heaven will reign over all the Earth; the Chariot will no longer sit above the Ark of the Covenant in the Temple of Jerusalem. It will be everywhere for everyone who is righteous.

Enoch gets a mission from God just like Ezekiel does[9] and it is similarly dire, about the horrible, violent behavior that will result in the destruction of the people who are doing the killing and other sins. Folks who were involved in Merkavah mysticism, who "rode the Chariot" (tried to achieve a vision of the Throne of God in their own place and time) didn't expect to receive a mission from God but instead simply wanted to experience the vision of the throne. On the other hand, it could be that the riders of the Chariot simply didn't discuss any mission they might have received but simply were hoping to receive the gift of prophecy. This would certainly fit with later schools of Jewish mysticism and prophecy, such as that of Abraham Abulafia, the 13th-century rabbi and founder of what is now called Prophetic Kabbalah.

Abulafia was a Spanish scholar of Kabbalah and an all-around character. He not only created a way to pronounce the Tetragrammaton (YHVH, the four-consonant Divine Name, whose vowels had been lost in time) but advised people on how to use the Name to achieve the gift of prophecy. For this he was excommunicated by rabbis in various locations (Judaism had no central authority to set dogma), but he ignored that and continued. He also believed that a trinity was at the center of Kabbalah and decided to go to Rome and present this as a proof of the validity of Judaism to the Pope, expecting the Pope to convert immediately. Instead, he was arrested, imprisoned, and held to be executed, but someone upstairs was watching, and the pope died before Abulafia's execution was held. His methods of pronouncing the Divine Name to achieve the gift of prophecy are still in use today.

People actually used the Ezekiel text for contemplation for their own ascension attempts, that is, trying to rise to Heaven to see the Chariot. Sometimes we are told this is done through the use of "seals," Divine Names, and other times the ascendant is simply led there by an angel. The ascension to the throne of Heaven described in Enoch 14 was inspired by the ascension in Ezekiel and is the oldest "ascension text" in Judaism outside of Ezekiel itself. By the time The Book of Enoch was written, people were already practicing ascension. Gershom Scholem, the prominent scholar of Jewish mysticism, argued that The Book of Enoch was the beginning of the practice of Merkavah (the vision of the Chariot), although many scholars disagree with that idea now and believe that Merkavah mysticism didn't start until later. Still, we are not going out on a limb to say that the people of Qumran, who treasured The Book of Enoch enough to make numerous copies of it, a task involving a lot of time and skill, obviously considered ascension an important idea, if not practice.

Nothing in the Hebrew Bible tells us that Enoch was a great human being, and there is no Enoch in the Prophets section of the Hebrew Bible. He was simply a human being. That's important because it means that The Book of Enoch implies that any person can ascend to Heaven simply by being righteous and by trying. We will see that this idea—that an ordinary human being can ascend to Heaven (and even stay there for three years)—will be highly attractive down through the ages to various religious or spiritual people, both Jews who wanted to attain the vision of the Chariot and Christians who saw Enoch's ascension and implied transformation into an angel as a way of explaining Jesus being both man and divine.

The Forbidden Knowledge of The Book of Enoch

CHAPTER TWO

Jewish History and Apocalyptic Works

There is not a lot of information available about Judaism in the 4th and 3rd centuries BCE, which is when the oldest sections of The Book of Enoch were written, mostly because there was so much turmoil in that time period—wars, for instance. Alexander the Great had conquered the region in 332 BCE, which led to a highly disruptive Hellenization[10] of Judaism and Israelite society.

At the same time, there was a revitalization of the sacrificial cult on account of the Second Temple being built soon after the Zadokite priesthood returned from Babylon in 538–515 BCE. We know that two sections of The Book of Enoch were written during that time: The Watchers and The Astronomical Book. These were originally separate books, and many scholars further believe that The Watchers was composed of at least two (Shemihazah and Asael) or even more ancient books or stories, which have been lost to us. The time between 513 BCE to 70 CE is called the Second Temple[11] period. The Book of Enoch as a whole, the result of at least five older books being compiled, is a product of this period.

Apocalyptic Works

Apocalyptic works were mostly written during the period after the return of a large group of the Jerusalemites from Babylonian exile in 538 BCE. A number decided to stay there and went on to write one version of the Talmud—the Babylonian Talmud as opposed to the Jerusalem Talmud. (The

Jerusalem Talmud was written in Aramaic in the Land of Israel (in Tiberias and Caesarea). It includes the same version of the Mishna as the Babylonian Talmud but then contains notes on the oral teachings of the Rabbis of the Land of Israel.) The apocalyptic works typically forecast some momentous event to happen after a particular length of time, and usually that event was equal to either a reset of society or a cataclysmic overturning of the old and institution of the new, perhaps even an end of the world. The Book of Enoch and Daniel both contain sections that are considered to be apocalyptic. The most famous Christian apocalypse is the Book of Revelation, written in Greek between 81–96 CE. It is now part of the Christian scriptures, although whether it should be part of the Christian canon has been controversial.

In the past, scholars believed that apocalyptic books were produced by the enormous social strains of the Maccabean rebellions (167–160 BCE), but we know now that at least a couple of the books that comprise The Book of Enoch were written long before that time.

Early History of Enoch

The Watchers (Enoch 1-36) and The Astronomical Book (Enoch 72–82) are the oldest Jewish religious works outside of the Hebrew Bible and the oldest examples of apocalyptic writing. They were most likely originally composed in the 4th through 3rd centuries BCE. Traditionally, studies of Enoch have considered The Watchers to be the oldest part (maybe because it is the only part that doesn't actually even mention Enoch), but nowadays more scholars say The Astronomical Book is the oldest section.

The entirety of The Book of Enoch had been put together (from five different books) at the beginning of the 2nd century BCE. When actual fragments of an Aramaic version of Enoch were found at Qumran between 1951–1976, there was proof of not only when it was written (based on the lettering, ink, and type of scroll it was written on) but that it was at least partially written in Aramaic. The only problem with this is that JT Milik, who found and published these fragments, perhaps added bits here and there and mistranslated some parts. Some Hebrew fragments from the part of the book relating to Noah have also been found at Qumran.

This is important because Hebrew was the national language of the Hebrew people until the exile to Babylon, where the elite of Jerusalem adopted a version of Aramaic (Jewish Babylonian Aramaic) that was one of the two primary languages of Babylon. They brought this version of Aramaic back to Jerusalem with them, following their return from exile, but nationalist forces, reacting to the imposition and growth of Hellenism, as mentioned earlier, began using Hebrew again. It's definitely possible time-wise that Enoch was originally composed in Hebrew.

Altogether, seven Aramaic copies of The Watchers, Book of Dreams, and Epistle of Enoch were found at Qumran. These copies were composed from late 200 BCE to the beginning of 100 BCE, with some having been copied during the time of Herod the Great (37 BCE–4 BCE). That would make some parts of Enoch older than Daniel, which was written in the 2nd century BCE and composed partly in Aramaic and partly in Hebrew. The Astronomical Book and The Watchers were available separately in the 3rd and 2nd centuries BCE in the Land of Israel. Scholars have concluded that The Book of Enoch as a whole was written in Judea in the Land of Israel. This is important because in the past, many believed that Enoch was written in Qumran, which is in the Judean Desert on the shores of the Dead Sea. However, Qumran didn't come into being until long after Enoch was written, so we know it didn't originate there; it was just a text that was often copied there. Fragments of all the parts of Enoch were found at Qumran except one: Similitudes, the last book included in Enoch.

The Watchers, one of the two oldest parts of The Book of Enoch, was written in Judea right after Alexander the Great conquered it in 333–323 BCE and during the wars of the Diadochi —those who succeeded Alexander, in 323–302 BCE. The Watchers doesn't show much anti-Hellenism, as the resistance to Hellenism had not yet had much time to take hold and remake Judaism in its own image. These were tough times, but nowhere near as difficult as the time period that produced the later texts, The Book of Dreams and the Epistle of Enoch, which came about around the time of the Maccabean Revolt. At that time, Antiochus IV[12] completely disrupted the Temple cult and outlawed traditional Judaic practices, probably with help from some of the Jewish elites who were influenced by Hellenism. You can imagine the divisions that existed in that situation.

The Watchers was most likely produced by the scribes of the Temple of Jerusalem. The influence of this work would grow for both Jews and, later, Christians, especially in terms of how they conceptualized the world before the Flood. Most readers did not accept its idea that evil came into the world due to the actions of a group of angels, but the story of the descent of the Watchers was important to Jews interpreting Genesis 6:1-4, especially before the rise of Rabbinism.[13] The Jesus Movement also embraced The Book of Enoch, and early Christians took up the book as well. The Book of Enoch kept on being popular with early Christians, who took it in new directions that were pertinent to their belief system, focusing more on the figure of Enoch as one of individual salvation. They also gave much more importance to the demonic aspects of the Watchers and the Nephilim.

The Rabbis abandoned The Book of Enoch. They said that the sons of God were humans, not angels, and that Enoch was just a human being; he had never been physically lifted up to Heaven. They argued that the statement about God taking him up to Heaven only meant that Enoch had died a normal human death. The rejection of this book was one of the ways that the Rabbis drew a line between themselves and the Jesus Movement. They didn't even mention Enoch until after the Talmud was completed, which was several centuries later.

Around that same time, the third and fourth centuries CE, Christians began rejecting The Book of Enoch also, especially once the Roman Empire was Christianized. They kept it out of the canon of Christian scripture and they no longer interpreted Genesis 6:1–4 as being about angels. Enoch was still being read by Christians in Ethiopia and Egypt, but because Christians attacked it, it was "lost" in the West for centuries. In Christianity, it was preserved mostly in quotes, and in Judaism by movements that had more of an interest in magic and mysticism, such as the Hasidei Ashkenaz.[14]

Is Enoch Fringe? No.

In the past, scholars thought that all the early Jewish apocalypses were written by groups that were cut off from the mainstream of Judaism. These imagined groups were seen as anti-establishment, maybe people who'd gathered around a particular prophet and who were engaged in attaining and keeping hidden knowledge secret and out of the hands of the mainstream and the authorities.

Powerlessness was considered to have been central to these books, the implication being that when you have no power, your imagination lifts you out of how pinched your life is. Daniel, which is partly an apocalyptic work, did arise out of oppression, and we might say that Revelation also arose from disenfranchisement, but this doesn't apply to all sorts of other apocalyptic texts. Various people in modern times thought that visionaries passed down their wisdom secretly; this was due mostly to the influence of the famous scholar of Jewish mysticism, Gershom Scholem, who thought secret knowledge that was passed down orally was responsible for how particular ideas might turn up in Jewish writing either without any apparent predecessor or seemingly unconnected in any clear way to the past history of ideas in Judaism. The problem with orally passed-down knowledge is that there is no way to say what it was or if it ever existed, and "oh, it was passed down orally and secretly" is not proof.

People have looked for the missing evidence that, for instance, the two oldest parts of Enoch—The Watchers and The Astronomical Book—were the products of even a particular group, and they didn't find it. There is no particular terminology that identifies these two parts of Enoch with any group that we know. No special terms are used that don't also occur in plenty of other texts.

The other issue we run into when we try to figure out where a particular text came from is that we don't really know, most of the time, who wrote it, edited it, copied it, read it, responded to it, interpreted it, and preserved it. We can't even look at whether a text was made part of the Jewish or Christian canon and say, "it wasn't included, so it's edgy" or "it was included, so it's not problematic." Being outside the canon doesn't mean the work is anti-authoritarian or full of secret knowledge. It might be, but just being outside the canon doesn't make it so. We should be wary of the idea that because a work is outside of the mainstream that it contains secrets or is anti-authoritarian. A work's secrets might not even be apparent on its surface, or the keys to unlock its meaning might have been lost, their context forgotten.

We can't even claim that Enoch was a Gnostic[15] text; the Gnostics never mentioned it, and people who attacked Gnostic Christianity wrote about Enoch positively. In fact, the Christians who wrote about it the most were dry-as-toast, rational chronographers who were interested primarily in simply recording history.

Oral History

In the past, many academic scholars, who had already had training researching stories from the Hebrew Bible and attempting to find the "original" version of such stories, tried to do the same with the story of the Watchers. Looking for this original story also fed the idea that The Book of Enoch was shot through with secret knowledge that had been passed on only orally—secrets spoken quietly by a teacher to the students who were ready to receive those secrets. Judaism does have a powerful oral tradition and has since ancient times, but that doesn't mean that every single text has such a tradition to prop it up, or that this spoken knowledge is secret or lost. For us, the secret and forbidden knowledges in Enoch are outlined for us out loud in the text itself. What's more, oral and written traditions are very much woven together in ancient Judaism. We have to imagine how books were produced. For instance, a rich patron might decide that they want to dictate a story they've created or heard or some other sort of text to a scribe.

Remember that most people, even those who were wealthy, were not literate in ancient societies. Books were generally not read silently by a single person in private; instead, they were read aloud to groups or even, like the Torah, in public. The listeners generally interacted with what was read by asking questions, having discussions, and arguing, so there was nothing passive about listening. A text copied down by a scribe could be something the speaker might have dreamed, or a story they had heard. We don't have to conclude that because something is written down that it's basically dead and doesn't have any juice left in it anymore. Instead, we should think of these texts as being part of a changing fabric of speech and writing. We can see this especially with Hekhalot texts, where there's so much variation between manuscripts of the "same" text that we can't even tell which one is the "original" or even whether it's a compilation of various texts. This slipperiness really fits with how these ancient texts "acted"—we can see it all over in the Hebrew Bible where various versions of the same story might be told.

Furthermore, The Book of Enoch was popular with all sorts of groups during Second Temple Judaism. Everyone from folks in the Jesus Movement to strictly establishment Temple scribes read it and made use of it, and most of them believed it was actually written by Enoch.

The acceptance of The Book of Enoch only began to change a few centuries later, around the 2nd century CE. After the destruction of the Temple of Jerusalem, a movement of Jews who believed that study of the Torah could replace the sacrificial cult arose. These people abandoned Enoch as inauthentic and problematic with respect to its depiction of angels involving themselves in sin. Early Christians and those Jews who believed in Jesus as the Messiah still hadn't rejected The Book of Enoch at that time and they liked the story of the descent of the angels (who wouldn't?). This only changed as the Adam and Eve story of how evil came to the world (that humans created evil) took over. The only serious problem that early Christian writers had with Enoch was that they thought the claim that Enoch had written it was false, but since it is mentioned in Christian

Jewish History and Apocalyptic Works

Scripture (Jude) and writings, it gained validity. It was not unusual for Enoch to be bound together with Christian writings into books. Quotes and excerpts were also included by Christian writers like Syncellus.[16] Still, it only became canonical in the Ethiopian Christian Church.

Versions of Enoch

One thing to keep in mind about Enoch (and other ancient books) is that there were probably multiple versions of it—not just in terms of which books were included in it (we know, for instance, that Similitudes was *not* part of The Book of Enoch that was found at Qumran; it was added on later) but also in terms of chunks of text missing or added, words changed, plot elements shifted, and more. This was pretty much normal, and once again I want to point out that this kind of fluidity was more or less expected and apparently even valued. So literal readings of any ancient texts or approaches to them that value not one word being changed or that some very particular meaning can be extracted from a reading, and *only* that meaning, would be out of keeping with how the people who wrote these texts meant them to be received. The Watchers alone had multiple authors and editors.

We already know that people did not hesitate to write under the name of biblical figures to give their writing more validity and so their writing might be interpreted as a supplement to the Torah. It was also not just one sect or circle or geographic area that created these books. At the time Enoch was written (stretched over several centuries), Jews were accepting of differences in versions of sacred writings. This will be surprising to modern-day folks who are used to receiving sacred texts as frozen in time. It's more like these texts were written in water than carved in stone.

Over the years, The Book of Enoch slid from being seen by at least some as holy scripture to be more like explanatory footnotes or material to fill gaps in the information in the Torah.

Because nowadays we tend to see writings outside of the canon as invalid or unimportant, perhaps fraudulent, perhaps as suppressed secret truth, we might automatically think that people in the ancient world saw them that way too. But for one thing, The Book of Enoch and other books existed before any canon was formed, so Enoch didn't have outsider status to people back then. Also, even when canons began to be formed, there were people who rejected the very idea of a canon or simply believed that The Book of Enoch should be part of it. In fact, The Watchers and The Astronomical Book are older than Daniel, which is in the canon. Generally, though, they would not automatically approach Enoch as if it were suppressed.

We have proof that The Book of Enoch existed in Aramaic, and it was from there that it was translated into Greek and then into Ethiopic. It probably was originally written in Hebrew, but we don't know how it looked in its original form(s). These are mysteries. The way it appears now might well be quite different from its original version(s). We shouldn't let that bother us, however. The Greek versions were probably created by Hellenized Jews in the first century BCE.

In contrast to other versions of The Book of Enoch, the Ethiopic translation was created by Christians for Christians. This translation was made some time between approximately 350 CE, when the Aksumite kingdom[17] adopted Christianity, and when that kingdom gradually lost its power in the 500s CE. The section of Enoch called Similitudes (also known as The Book of Parables, chapters 37–51) is part of the holy book *Mashafa Milad*, which also contains Jubilees. (The Book of Jubilees is an ancient Hebrew text. It is considered to have been written between 160–150 BCE. It tells the same story as Genesis and much the same story as The Book of Enoch, but with Moses, who isn't mentioned in The Book of Enoch, at the center.) Enoch remains included in the canon of the Ethiopic Orthodox Tewahedo Church today.

The Similitudes section was not found at Qumran and apparently was written in the first century CE, probably by a Jewish Christian. Christians have often focused on this section of Enoch because of its depiction of the "Son of Man," the book's name for a supernatural messiah figure who would oversee the Final Judgment of humankind. The version of Enoch presently used in the Ethiopic Orthodox Tewahedo Church is different from the version that was brought back from Ethiopia in 1821 by professor of theology and translator Richard Laurence; apparently the version in the Bible of Emperor Haile Selassie is sometimes called a corrupt version because it's a *targum*. A targum is a particular sort of paraphrase for religious writings, mostly ancient Jewish ones of parts of the Hebrew Bible. *Targumim* (plural of targum) combine quotes from the sacred text with commentary and expansions on the stories in the text it's retelling. The paraphrases, commentaries, quotes, and stories are all run together, so a targum is by no means a word-for-word rendering of the original text. Targumim typically add really interesting perspectives to the canonical holy scripture. I highly recommend checking them out. They are quite engaging and burst apart any ideas commonly held today that Judaism was an authoritarian religion allowing only one central voice demanding obedience.

The influence of the Ethiopian Church in the West was not great, especially after the Muslim Conquest of North Africa and the Middle and Near East in the 600s CE, which essentially cut Ethiopia off from the Church centers of Rome (Catholic) and Constantinople (Eastern Orthodox), but it maintained connections with Coptic Orthodox churches in Egypt and continues to be strong today.

The Beta Israel, a group of over 100,000 Jews of Ethiopian descent who now primarily live in Israel, also have The Book of Enoch as part of their canon. They are the only Jewish denomination that does.

Most early Enochic literature was basically lost to the West from the early Middle Ages until the Early Modern period. In Western Europe, the entire text of Enoch was lost. Excerpts from Enoch were preserved in the chronographical writings (basically, theological histories in the form of expanded timelines) of Christianity and Byzantium. For decades, there were rumors in Europe that the full text of Enoch still existed in Ethiopia, and the "lost" book was finally rediscovered by the Scottish explorer James Bruce in 1773. The Ethiopic version of Enoch was brought to Western

Europe in 1821 and helped stimulate interest in Christianity's Judaic background. It was called Enoch to distinguish it from the Slavonic version of The Book of Enoch, which was renamed 2 Enoch in order to keep them separate. A Greek translation of part of 1 Enoch was discovered in 1886. Even before the translation of Enoch was printed in Europe, however, excerpts were available that were published in journals and were available to people like William Blake and Joseph Smith. On the one hand, we hear about how Enoch was lost for centuries, but on the other hand, bits and pieces of it appeared here and there and had impact. The translation of the book we today call Enoch is a combination of the Ge'ez, Greek, and Aramaic versions, with primacy usually given to the Aramaic, since this is the oldest. Some Hebrew fragments of the original have also been found.

CHAPTER THREE

Giants, Demons, and Babylon

We might look at The Book of Enoch's relationship to Babylon in terms of the fact that some see the book as a reaction against the Zadokite priesthood's corruption and arrogance after their return from Babylon, from which they brought their Babylonian wives and religious customs that they incorporated into the rites at the Temple. I will focus on this issue below. We know that late Mesopotamian culture influenced Jewish Aramaic writings, but here I'd like to bring up a theory that the Watchers are a stand-in for a particular type of Babylonian clergy that the Zadokite priesthood and other members of the Jerusalem elite including Temple scribes experienced in exile in Babylon.

In Late Babylonian society, exorcists (known as *asipu* or "incantation priests") were professionals associated with the Babylonian temple. They worked with magic herbalism, astrology, and astronomy with respect to herbs as well as conducting exorcisms. The Babylonian exorcists developed a practice of magical herbalism (often called "root-cutting" to distinguish it from purely medicinal herbalism), including cataloging the most magically appropriate times to harvest medicinal plants and how to treat injured, sick, or cursed people. They also cast or removed spells. In addition, they knew astronomy, how to divine using celestial and terrestrial objects, and how the stars influenced plants and people. They didn't practice the metal-working, goldsmithing, or work with precious stones and dyes that the Watchers did, but clearly some of what the Watchers knew seems to have been modeled on a number of the skills of the Babylonian exorcists.

The scribes and priests who had been exiled to Babylon weren't able to read the cuneiform writing that was still in use in the temple of Babylon, but at the time, the temple in Babylon itself had begun to use Babylonian Aramaic because it was far easier to master than cuneiform writing. The exiled scribes and priests acquired Babylonian Aramaic in Babylon and brought it back to Israel in the form of Jewish Babylonian Aramaic. The Jewish exiles also returned with some of the astronomical and astrological knowledge of the Babylonians as well as the Babylonian calendar, which ended up being quite problematic, since the original Judaic calendar was sun-based, not moon-based like the Babylonian calendar.

One of the "secrets" the Watchers shared with humans was how to interpret the signs of thunder. The Israelites had a system of divination where thunder was meaningful when heard during various signs of the zodiac, but in the Babylonian divination system, thunder heard in certain months had particular meanings (those same month names were later imported into the Jewish calendar, where they remain today). Yes, the Greeks had a system of reading the signs of thunder that was similar to the Babylonian one, but it didn't come into being until the Byzantine era, which was centuries later (395–1453 CE).

Certain aspects of what Enoch is described as seeing during his various heavenly journeys follow a pattern that is similar to descriptions of kingdom displays in ancient Near East writings. Kingdom displays were a sort of set way of describing a kingdom's riches, especially in terms of the palace treasures, throne, treasure houses, and such. These occurred in writings of the Near East, especially Babylonian.

Other Mesopotamian influences that strike others as clear maybe aren't really there. One is the comparison of what Enoch describes when he goes to the western regions where he sees beings like flaming fire that nevertheless have a human shape (1 Enoch 17:1–2). This might recall for us the Cherubim with their fiery swords who guard the gate to the Garden of Eden, following the expulsion of Adam and Eve. Some have said that these Cherubim are like the scorpion-men that guard Mount Mashu in the Epic of Gilgamesh.[19] But compare for yourself: the Cherubim are Fire spirits who guard the Garden of Eden (which is in the east, whence the Sun rises) and the scorpion men, as scorpions, are Earth spirits (or at best, Mars-ruled spirits) who guard the gates to the Underworld, where the sun goes at the end of the day. There doesn't seem to be any sort of parallel there, beyond their role of guardianship.

Other aspects of The Book of Enoch seem to have some relationship to Mesopotamian mythology, like the astronomical theories in the Book of the Luminaries,[20] the map of the world that is taken for granted in some parts of Enoch, and some patterns in common between Enoch as the seventh generation from Adam like the seventh king stories in ancient Mesopotamia.[21]

Just when we think that maybe there might be some parallels between Israelite and Babylonian imagery and stories, we see that perhaps they have nothing in common.

Giants and Demons

While I agree that the Watchers might on some level be the authors' critique of the class of Babylonian exorcists—the Watchers, at least those associated with Shemihazah, practiced all the same arts as the Babylonian exorcists—there's another assertion about the Nephilim, the destructive giants that cause havoc on Earth, that claims they are patterned on the Babylonian demons known as *utukku*. (Utukku is the plural; the singular form is *udug*.) The only distinctive physical feature of the Nephilim we get is that they are very big and tall. We can conclude that otherwise they look like human beings, because if they didn't, The Book of Enoch would have remarked on it. In contrast, the utukku are described as tall and having big voices, but they have no faces—they look like a dark shadow surrounded by light, and they are poisonous.

Some descriptions of the utukku are that they are nameless and formless, which is definitely not similar to the Nephilim—unless we want to talk about the spirits of the Nephilim that are allowed to continue on

Earth after the Flood. But we know nothing at all about those remnants of the Nephilim except that they tempt people to worship idols. While they are still flesh, the Nephilim attack, kill, and eat people and each other; the utukku make people and animals sick but don't eat them. They are violent, but they don't fight wars or eat people alive like the Nephilim did. (They did, however, eat dead people.)

The biggest difference between the Nephilim and the utukku is that the latter are sometimes good and sometimes bad. They are more like daimons than demons. Daimons were a Greek conception of spirits who were lesser than gods and might sometimes be both mortal and divine. They were also sometimes identified as the souls of great men of the past and were generally viewed as protective, which would certainly be a huge difference between them and the Nephilim. So at least on that level, there doesn't seem to be any possible comparison.

Several scholars have compared the Nephilim to warrior-kings, as sometimes the word used to describe them is Giborim,[22] rather than Nephilim. I think what is missing from that comparison is the recognition that ancient texts that are compiled of various other works written in other places and times will not be homogeneous or consistent. There will be inconsistencies, plots that are unfinished, the same story with different endings or characters, similar descriptions and even names provided to completely different characters, and more. Just remember that the biblical account of the creation of human beings is first described in Genesis as God making human beings, both male and female (Genesis 1:27), while a second, more famous story has God creating Adam out of clay and Eve from one of Adam's ribs while he slept (Genesis 2:7, 2:21–22). Pretty big difference in an important story!

That is why the occasional description of the Nephilim as Giborim, much less the Greek translation of Nephilim as *Grigori* (giants), isn't bothersome to me. The Hebrew Bible is not a history book or a novel. It is a jagged, cut-and-sewn-together text made by a variety of people who had different intentions over a span of many years. We must always expect inconsistencies and not get hung up on them or believe that contradictions invalidate the text as a whole. This is not a straw man for an argument about the veracity of the divine. It is an incredible book that was created by human beings who were divinely inspired. Humans are contradictory. We can relish that instead of seeing it as a flaw. In my opinion, our inconsistency and contradiction are exactly part of what makes us not only survivors but also interesting and creative.

The utukku were originally messengers of the gods' anger, but they don't belong to any pantheon. They were never worshiped in any cult and never had devotees who built them a temple. They have more in common with restless, destructive windstorms than living beings. They can perpetrate great violence, but they are much more liable to sneak into a house, lurk in the street, and loiter around homes looking for human targets whom they can terrorize and make ill. They can even pry humans loose from the protection of their patron god, turning them away from the gods who protect them like from the clasp of lovers, by leading them away. Because they receive no offerings from worshipers, they are resentful and prey upon the society that excludes them. They ruin good land and stunt plants. They make new fruits fall from the trees so they can never ripen. They trample what ripe fruits there are. They hurt animals. They attack cities and villages, killing people and then eating them.

The utukku cannot be propitiated because they are not connected to any worship system, but they can be bribed. The job of the temple exorcists was to dislodge utukku from the body of someone whom they had sickened. They'd bribe the utukku to leave and go to the land of the dead by outfitting them for the journey with shoes, clothes, food, drink, and leather pouches to hold it all. This is exactly what the temple exorcists would do to outfit the souls of the dead for their journey to the Underworld. After being exorcised, these demons linger around empty places, hoping another person will come by for them to infest. Although these critters are pestiferous, I don't think their behavior holds a candle to the murderous destructiveness of the Nephilim. I think they have nothing in common at all. For one thing, the utukku target individuals and seem to be readily ousted by the temple exorcists. In contrast, the Nephilim devour the entire world and

Giants, Demons, and Babylon

only a catastrophic event can destroy them. To compare the utukku with the Nephilim is to compare a schoolyard bully with a terrorist organization.

Second Temple Judaism and Enochic Judaism

Numerous sects existed in Judaism during the Second Temple period, and some scholars have argued that Enochic Judaism was one of them. So, what is Enochic Judaism?

Basically, it's a type of Judaism that takes Enoch, along with Jubilees, Testaments of the Twelve Patriarchs,[23] and 4 Ezra[24] as their primary texts. Enochic Judaism might have been a sect that used Enoch as a lens to focus on wisdom literature with science and mysticism as its main topics and perhaps existed during the Hellenistic and Roman periods of Jewish history. They were not thought to be an apocalyptic group, because of these four texts, only Enoch is apocalyptic. Two of these texts, Enoch and Jubilees, influenced early Christianity, so some have linked Enochic Judaism with Christianity. The problem with that is there were various groups that prized Enoch that had no connection with Christianity; in fact, people who belonged to no particular sect of Judaism—who weren't very attentive to the sacrificial cult and probably didn't worship at any local altars, who didn't belong to any sects, like the Essenes, a Jewish religious group that existed in Judea from the second century BCE to the first century CE, used Enoch, so it was far from limited to one sect.[25]

Gabriele Boccaccini, professor of Second Temple Judaism and early Christianity, is the strongest voice for Enochic Judaism. His teacher, Paolo Sacchi, believed that Jewish apocalyptic literature was about the supernatural origin of sin, in particular in the form of the story of the descent of the Watchers that is included in Enoch 6–11. Even though Daniel is also an apocalyptic book, Boccaccini pointed out that it doesn't address the origin of sin on Earth and that therefore, to his mind, it can't be put into the category of Jewish apocalyptic works. Like Sacchi, he argues that all Jewish apocalyptic works contain some version of how evil arrived among human beings. He considered, like most modern scholars, that the books that comprise Enoch were written from the fourth century BCE all the way to the first century CE.

During this period of five hundred years, the central idea that he thinks unites all the parts of Enoch is that they describe how humans were not responsible for evil appearing on Earth but that instead, evil existed not only before human beings could make choices (when we were still living in the Garden of Paradise) but even before human beings existed. I think we can see that this idea is a bit beyond the Watchers' story, where evil comes down from Heaven specifically because of human beings existing, even though humans are not responsible for that evil in The Book of Enoch. This extra-human evil corrupted human nature.

A number of scholars agree with Boccaccini that Enoch represents a particular strand of Judaism during the late third and early second centuries BCE. Most people in this group see the folks at Qumran as the center of Enochic Judaism, but we must remember that some of the material that's part of these texts, like The Watchers and The Astronomical Book, the oldest sections of Enoch, were written before the Qumran community was founded. Clearly, then, those books are reflecting Jewish traditions from before the 3rd century BCE or even earlier and then, when the Essenes of Qumran ran across them, those texts spoke to their concerns. Some think that the groups who wrote and popularized The Book of Enoch and associated writings were the parents of the Dead Sea sect that made Qumran their home. Still, the people who collected the Dead Sea Scrolls did not reject the Mosaic Torah; in fact, the Hebrew Bible is also central to that community. Because the community did not reject the Hebrew Bible and Mosaic Law, some say that really there was no such thing as the Essenes.

However, J.T. Milik, one of the most important translators of Enoch, who worked with the Aramaic fragments of Enoch found in the caves at Qumran, had a theory that Enoch functioned as a Pentateuch for the Essenes, whom he equated with the people who lived communally at Qumran. Instead of including Similitudes (chapters 37–71), which was never found at Qumran and which most believe was written by Christians

Giants, Demons, and Babylon

35

later on,[26] he included The Book of Giants[27] as the fifth book in Enoch, although the entirety of Giants was not found at Qumran either.

He also pointed out that The Astronomical Book found at Qumran was twice as long as the Ethiopic version, which to him implied that it was highly important to the people of Qumran. Likewise, Milik considered that Enoch, a heavenly scribe, sage, and seer, served as a substitute for Moses (who possessed the same aspects) in the Qumran group. That version of Enoch, however, was not confined to Qumran—many Jews believed that about Enoch but didn't therefore reject Mosaic law or the Pentateuch (the first five books and the oldest sections of the Hebrew Bible: Genesis, Exodus, Leviticus, Numbers, and Deuteronomy).

The thing is that just because there are five main works in the Ethiopic version of Enoch doesn't mean that Jews, Greeks, or Ethiopians considered it to be another Pentateuch. Also, the community of Qumran had good reasons not to keep a copy of the Similitudes around—it describes the sun and the moon as having equal roles and jobs, whereas Qumran considered the sun way more important. I think this was because the original Temple calendars were solar, not lunar.

Mosaic Law

Mosaic Law is not important in The Book of Enoch. This might be startling, but we often forget that Mosaic law was not the starting point of Judaism, no matter how important it eventually became. Mosaic Law consisted of the Ten Commandments and all the commandments that unfolded from them and that occur in Leviticus and Deuteronomy, such as no lighting a fire on the Sabbath, how sacrifices should be conducted in the Temple of Jerusalem, laws of ritual purity, what is ritually pure to eat, how the Temple should be furnished, which feast days should be observed, rules of property and inheritance, and more. For a long time (even now, for that matter), some of the other strands of Judaism did not think the Law of Moses was anything like primary; some even considered that it didn't matter. The Dead Sea Scrolls treat the Books of Genesis and Exodus as sources for stories and wisdom rather than as prescriptive law. The first books to seriously talk about Halakhah are The Temple Scroll[28] and Jubilees, which came about after the Maccabean revolt.

At that time (circa 167–134 BCE), various sects were emerging within Judaism, as a result of urbanization, greater literacy in the population, and political criticisms of the rulers after independence from the Seleucid Empire (based in Syria) after the Maccabean Revolt. The rise of sects in turn might well be the cause of increasing importance of Halakhah, as the Law might be taken as some kind of ultimate determiner of who was "right" in sectarian disputes. At any rate, the Law was something that people could point to as a group of concrete rules. We can see this in the way the Essenes separated from Judaism; it wasn't that they rejected Mosaic law (although they weren't all that interested in focusing on it—their own Aramaic texts were not about Mosaic Law) but that they didn't like the way the Pharisees interpreted it.

Some scholars have thought that because The Book of Enoch has nothing in it about the giving of the Law at Sinai that it would logically become a central text for a group that rejected Toraitic law. Toraitic law refers to the law written in the Torah (the written law) as opposed to the oral law of the Talmud. But since The Book of Enoch is set in Enoch the man's time, which was long before Moses, it makes sense that Moses is not mentioned.

Various other texts exist that don't mention the books of Moses either. In fact, the so-called Enochic Jews did abide by much of Mosaic Law, and we don't find that they were part of theoretical disputes on the subject. In fact, one theory about why they went out to Qumran to establish a community was that they thought the Law, especially commandments related to purity, was not abided by strictly enough in Jerusalem.

While we know that the people of Qumran didn't write Enoch, they did make multiple copies of it, which means that it was important to them. One of the notable aspects of Enoch is that even though it interprets Genesis 6:1–4, it never makes any mention of the Mosaic covenant. It wasn't until the Hasmonean[29] rulers of the Land of Israel (c. 140 BCE–37 BCE) that Halakhic issues became important in texts of the time.

One reason various sects of Second Temple Judaism might not have been all that interested in discussing Halakhah is that most of the great law codes of the ancient Near East were not about creating or aiding the practice of law. Instead, the law was decided by the king, as we see in the stories of King Solomon making rulings for people who came before him for that purpose, such as the two women who wanted him to decide whose baby it was in The Judgment of King Solomon. Even in ancient Israel, the Law might be for teaching purposes or to be ritually read and not so much "you can't do this." This makes sense of the Talmudic approach to the Law, where instead of seeing commandments as the ultimate and last word, commandments are to be interpreted and can potentially be modified out of existence by groups of rabbis. It also kind of kicks the Torah-True or Fundamentalist approaches to the Hebrew Bible into a cocked hat, as the saying goes. The Torah-True folks believe that we must take everything in the Torah as literal truth, including commandments like "Kill the next Amalekite you see." The fact is that even in ancient times, no one took the commandments literally; the Law was subject to modification.

Eventually, the Halakhah *did* come to be prescriptive. Scholars don't know exactly when that happened, partly because there are some big gaps in history. It might have occurred around the time of Josiah's reform,[30] Ezra's reform,[31] or during the Hellenistic period. However, even if we take, for instance, Josiah's reform as the time when Halakhah begins to be seen as prescriptive, when Josiah himself is criticized for violating the Law, he doesn't rely on what's written in the book as the final word; instead, he consults a prophetess, Huldah, in order to get the specifics about how the Law applies to this particular case. Instead of acting as a lawyer or judge who interprets the Law, she asks the Divine directly what it means in the particular instance, and she tells Josiah. So even then the Law was not taken as the last word; instead, a divinely inspired person, male or female, could reveal what God had to say about the application of that law.

One of the distinctive aspects of The Book of Enoch is that the main figure in this apocalypse is not Moses or one of the Patriarchs of the Hebrew Bible but instead Enoch, who is otherwise a very minor biblical character. Also, the core of Enoch is judgment of those who sin, not illustrations of the Law. Some say that this implies a rejection of Mosaic law (and it did come to mean something like that for Christians later on). However, in the early 2nd century BCE, the Torah was not at the center of Judaism for everyone, even for those who believed it was important; they might see it as one wisdom text among many others. Those who wrote The Book of Enoch simply didn't acknowledge Mosaic law, perhaps in order to make the point that the story and its moral—that God will punish sin and reward the righteous—was intended as a lesson for all humanity, not just for the Israelites. This too will be a reason why Christians initially embrace Enoch.

Giants, Demons, and Babylon

CHAPTER FOUR

Magic and Enoch
at Qumran

The Book of Enoch and Qumran both were about purity, but perhaps Qumran rejected the Zadokite priests' arrogant perspective on purity and instead went for the purity of The Book of Enoch, which was not about Zadokite rules. We know that the concept of purity was very important in Second Temple Judaism. Since generally it was considered that God lived in the Temple of Jerusalem, it made sense that the closer one lived to the Temple, the stricter the laws of purity should be. In those days there were two types of purity issues—ritual purity and moral purity. Ritual impurity was short-term and caused by things you couldn't help, like sex that was permitted, the burial of the dead, menstruation, or ejaculating during a dream. Someone else could be contaminated with ritual impurity by touch, and it required bathing, waiting a certain time period, or making a sacrifice at the Temple.

Moral impurity was more dire. It came about because of sins like sex that was not permitted, killing, or worshiping idols, but it could not be passed on to someone else. It was yours alone and could only be gotten rid of through the appropriate atonement or by being punished.

As long as the Temple was standing, the priests would be the ones to help people rid themselves of this kind of impurity. For the most part, those priests would have been Zadokites and Sadduccees, their descendants. The Zadokites came to dominate Judaism after the Maccabean

Revolt, and subsequent writings like Daniel and Jubilees tended to include Moses and Mosaic Law.

Both Enochic and Zadokite Judaism were very interested in purity and the calendar, but there were great differences between them. Once the Second Temple was built, the Zadokites considered that divine order had been restored and God was once again a presence in the Temple. But the Enochic Jews thought the rebuilt Temple was corrupted and that a true, pure temple would be rebuilt in the future and by the Divine, not by human beings.

If the people of Qumran thought the Temple was impure, what did they have as an alternative? They intended to create a center of what they considered to be authentic purity at their commune in Qumran. In order to be made a full member of the community, one had to abide by many rules regarding purity and go through much ritual purification.

How did the Temple get to the point that it was considered corrupt by the people who left Jerusalem to found the community at Qumran? This happened due to the actions of Antiochus Epiphanes. He sacrificed a pig, an unclean animal, at the altar in the outer court of the Temple, sprinkled the holy books with pork broth, and forced the high priests to eat pork. He later had an altar to Zeus put into the outer court of the Temple in 167 BCE. For that he got the Maccabean Revolt. Judas Maccabeus cleansed and rededicated the Temple in 164 BCE. That was a positive event except for one thing—the Maccabees were not descended from Zadokite priests, so of course some thought they could not really purify the Temple and that they should not be running it. The Zadokite priests in particular were against it, but they lost. Some historians believe that these Zadokites retreated to the desert, where they formed their own community based on purity, and that they became known as the Essenes. One problem with this theory is that there were Essenes all over the Land of Israel, not just in this desert location.

Another perspective on why the people who formed Qumran left Jerusalem was that they tried to convince the Temple priesthood that the laws of purity should be extended beyond the temple complex, but this idea was rejected. Thus, they left to form a community that they thought would be purer in the desert.

One take on the Qumran community is that it was a branch of the Essenes but much more radical and marginal. Some scholars have thought that the Qumran community was composed of Zealots, Jesus Followers, or that it was just garden-variety Essenes.

The other issue is that there were Essenes before the so-called Antiochene Crisis. What they had in common with the Qumran community was similar views on determinism (that the divine determines everything in advance) and dualism (that there is the divine on one side and the demonic on the other). They both interpreted the Hebrew Bible in a similar way and had similar ideas of the doctrine of angels, and they believed that the Temple would be part of the Last Judgment. The Qumran community was the result of a split in the Essene movement due to differences in how the Law should be interpreted, especially with respect to purity, the calendar to be used to determine when festivals occurred, and how the worship at the Temple was to be conducted.

Some have argued that Qumran had roots (like the rest of the Essenes) in the tradition of apocalypse, but a few have said that they go back to Ezekielism and Enoch instead. Even so, we have no evidence that Qumran evolved from the people who wrote Enoch.

We can't say that the Qumran community rejected Mosaic Law when about a quarter of the manuscripts found there were from the Hebrew Bible.

Some of the Enochic literature used in Qumran were Jubilees, The Genesis Apocryphon,[32] and Giants. These were written before Qumran, but another document was probably written by them: The Damascus Document. This was written in Hebrew and fragments of it were found in modern times in Qumran and in the Cairo Geniza. It is a description of laws for the community of Qumran. It erects a set of special laws that apply to the Qumran community and damns the rest of the Jews in the land for not living by them. "Damascus" in the title might be a way of

Magic and Enoch at Qumran

referring to Babylon, although the city of Damascus was part of the Land of Israel during the reign of King David.

So why did people end up retreating to Qumran? Basically, because they didn't think the people around them were pious or pure enough. Some call the folks of Qumran sanctimonious, fanatical, arrogant, and more than a little controlling. They certainly expressed contempt for people who disagreed with their interpretations of Mosaic Law.

What struck me when reading about them was how much they seemed to have in common with the Hasidei Ashkenaz of medieval Germany, who also knew something about Enoch. The Hasidei Ashkenaz also had truck with angels, were very strict about their observance of the Law, and looked down on folks outside of their sect because they didn't think other people were pious enough. And they were arrogant enough to make golems, beings made from clay and animated by the use of Divine Names.

Gershom Scholem connected the Qumran community with Hekhalot, but more recent scholars think he was mistaken about that. I've studied some Hekhalot and from what I can see, Qumran doesn't have much to do with Hekhalot and neither does Enoch. It might seem so on the surface, since both Enoch and Hekhalot involve ascending to Heaven, but Hekhalot texts have a very set conception of the levels of Heaven and what is necessary for an individual to ascend them. In contrast, Enoch is able to ascend because an angel takes him there; there is no mention of any particular phrases or names to be spoken to the angels guarding each level of Heaven or seals to show them. One scholar has pointed out that Enoch's trip to Heaven can't be seen as a Hekhalot text because Enoch is a special case from the beginning—God lifted him up bodily to Heaven. Ascenders in Hekhalot are fully alive people. In the past, the Hekhalot ascension(s) were seen as something imaginary or to meditate upon; more recently, Hekhalot ascensions are viewed as sort of guidebooks for people who want to try ascending in whatever form it might take.

In the past, some scholars argued that the Essenes must have been influenced by the Neopythagoreans,[33] but the Essenes not only did not know Greek, they actually rejected Hellenism, seeing it as an attack on

Judaism and Israelite nationalism. They would not have been imitating anything the Neopythagoreans did even if they knew about it.

While Qumran might not have been practicing heavenly ascension like the later users of Hekhalot texts, they certainly had mystical and magical elements as part of their view of the world. Nor was the interest in magic and living with the angels a foreign influence; magic and working with angels was part of Second Temple Judaism.

Part of the liturgy at Qumran was The Songs of the Sabbath Sacrifice (aka Angelic Liturgy). The community of Qumran didn't write this document, but they obviously thought it was valuable. This work described various levels of Heaven but didn't include any sort of story; it didn't show or describe any particular character ascending to the heavens to see the throne of God. Instead, it simply described Heaven and the throne and how the angels acted and what they sang. It is not odd to think that when this text was read aloud to the people of Qumran, they joined in with the angelic songs of praise. This is done today in the Jewish liturgy, although no congregants believe that they are actually ascending, only that they are singing *Kadosh, kadosh, kadosh* ("Holy, holy, holy") as the angels do in Heaven. There is even a charming motion that is made with each "kadosh"—raising oneself on one's toes to be closer to Heaven.

It seems clear that the Qumran sect viewed the Temple of Jerusalem as corrupted and not a place where the Divine resided. They might well have seen their own community as a place pure enough to function as a location for the Divine to reside. That didn't mean that they thought they were at their own moment worthy of functioning as a metaphorical temple, and there was never any altar found in that place. The temple they envisioned was located in the future and would be built by God, not by people. In the view of the Qumran sect, this would happen after the Judgment Day.

There were both men and women at Qumran, and they had marriage, which involved a number of questions of purity. Qumran had a different view of what made people ritually impure (they included sin in that category, whereas normally sin made people *morally* impure, not ritually). They paid particular attention to lying, blasphemy, and idolatry (which

Magic and Enoch at Qumran

45

we will see is especially encouraged by the demons that the spirits of 10 percent of the Nephilim became after the Flood). They also blurred the border between ritual and moral purity in the other direction, asserting that ritual impurity from menstruation or ejaculation during dream was morally defiling instead of simply making a person ritually impure.

They considered outsiders to the community both ritually and morally unclean because outsiders didn't know the proper interpretation of the Hebrew Bible (that is, the Qumran interpretation) and because outsiders wouldn't or didn't submit to Qumran discipline. They held that only if all members of their community were pure would the Divine come to reside with them.

The Qumran community existed for over two hundred years, and the longer the community was apart from the mainstream, the stricter and more isolated they became.

Qumran and Hebrew

The language of Qumran and other religious communities of this time was Hebrew, even though many other people were using Aramaic. Hebrew was especially spoken by high status folk in these communities because it was thought that by using Hebrew they could communicate with divine spirits and pass on what they learned from such communication.

Documents written in Hebrew, Aramaic, Greek, and Nabatean were found at Qumran, so to some extent at least the people were multilingual. But about three quarters of the manuscripts found there were written in Hebrew. Hebrew was the native language of Israel in the time of the First Temple and even with the encroachment of Aramaic remained the written language. But there was a great revival of the Hebrew language in the 2nd century BCE that coincided with the upsurge of religious nationalism that accompanied the Maccabean Revolt. Hebrew was then written in paleo-Hebrew script, which we see printed on Hasmonean coins—and which the Qumran sect chose to use to write some of their own copies of the Hebrew Bible. Some say they used that script instead of the Mishnaic Hebrew of the Pharisees to set themselves off from the Pharisees. Others say that they wrote in Paleo-Hebrew simply to create another border between what they thought of as their higher purity and the lower level of purity of the rest of the Jews.

It was at around the second century BCE that Hebrew came to be referred to as the "holy tongue." Jubilees says that Abraham and his children were able to learn from the angels and from the ancient sages because they knew Hebrew, which was taught to them by an angel, and one day everyone would speak this holy tongue. You can see why Qumran would consider Hebrew vital; not only did they want to communicate with angels and to join in with the angels' rites in Heaven, but they believed that Hebrew would be *the* language after the Judgment. Since the Qumran community no longer had access to the Temple of Jerusalem, they would sing hymns in Hebrew together was a way to share the knowledge and activities of the angels.

Qumran and Magic

There are two aspects of the magical practices connected to Hekhalot/ Merkavah. One is ascending to Heaven, and the other is conjuring angels like the Sar Torah (The Prince of the Torah, a ritual practice to adjure an angel to come to the operator and give them knowledge of the Torah and the memory necessary to work with it). The Qumran sect's The Songs of the Sabbath Sacrifice is more like ascension than conjuration and uses the same kind of poetry as Merkavah texts.

One interesting take on Hekhalot texts is that they are not about uniting with the angels or the Divine—which is often an aspect of "high" magic in Western esotericism—but instead are about changing oneself to the point where one can be enthroned in Heaven, like Enoch was.

Hekhalot Rabbati, in the past seen as a mystical text and now more often viewed as a magical handbook, says that anyone who practices the text to mastery will be able to terrify their enemies, give them horrific skin diseases, and other attack magic. Not much mystical going on with that. There are sections of Hekhalot Rabbati that say that the reader can ascend to Heaven on their own, without the assistance of angels or the Divine, which is compared to having a ladder to Heaven in one's own house. Maybe not just any ordinary human being can achieve this ascension, but according to various texts, some humans have done it. Hekhalot implies that anyone who reads the book can attempt the journey and possibly succeed. How *exactly* one ascends is not precisely spelled out in Hekhalot; instead, there are rituals that describe how to prepare for meeting in person an angel one has called down to earth in order to teach or give the gift of memory. It's unclear whether the ascension procedure was transmitted orally or whether you just had to work it out for yourself. I suspect the latter.

Enoch After the Destruction of the Temple

After the desecration of the Temple by Antiochus IV, it had to be purified. The timing of the festivals also had to be recalculated because using the lunar calendar threw off all the dates. Subsequently, due to the rise of Hellenism and many intrigues among the high priests, the rise of non-Zadokite priests in the Temple because of the Maccabean Revolt and then the corrupt power of the Hasmoneans after the Revolt, many Jews wondered what the true nature of a chosen people was, how should or could they relate to other nations, and what might be the bases of political and religious authority. What's more, greater tumult in society occurred all the way up to the Bar Kokhba rebellion (Jewish-Roman war, 132–136 CE) due to the simultaneous growth of various religious sects from the Pharisees, the Sadducees, the Essenes, and the Jesus Movement.

Gradually during this period, the use of the story of Adam and Eve to explain the origin of evil in the world grew; no longer was evil considered to have arisen from supernatural sources like angels.

With the rise of Rabbinism, The Book of Enoch began to disappear from any mention in Jewish texts and only persevered for a while among Christian groups. After the Bar Kokhba rebellion was smashed by the Romans, both post-Temple Judaism and proto-orthodox Christianity moved apart from each other as they began to shape who they were in a very much changed world.

CHAPTER FIVE

Enoch and the
Canon in Judaism

There's disagreement about when the canon was formed in Judaism. Some argue that it came about during the time of the Maccabees, and others say it began to be formed after the destruction of the Second Temple and didn't become fully closed to new additions until many years after that, maybe even centuries later. Bava Batra (a volume of the Talmud) 14b does give a list of the order of the books of the Prophets[35] and Wisdom or Writings[36] that were kept in the Ark in the Second Temple. Of course, Enoch is not on that list, but what does that really mean?

We have to remember that even if a canon existed, that does not mean that the people who wrote and used works that didn't end up in the canon were on some kind of fringe or not part of the mainstream, although it's true that all sorts of texts that would become non-canonical were found at, for instance, Qumran. All kinds of Jews shared various texts as the core of Judaism without there even being a canon. That we have no evidence of a canon in Judaism prior to the destruction of the Second Temple might well imply that people just didn't care about creating a canon.

What's interesting is that as people began to want a canon, they also began to reject deviation in various versions of the holy books and wanted some kind of standardization of these texts. You can see how the ancients' idea of how a sacred text could be contradictory to itself—like contain two versions of how humans were created—had begun to lose favor and that it became more important to people that a sacred text be more internally consistent. Keep in mind that books were hand copied, which was done by different scribes at the request of different individuals or groups; there was plenty of variation between copies of the same book.

In Rabbinics and Later

The Pharisees during the Second Temple period had set up study houses where ordinary Jews could access and learn about sacred texts without having to go through the Temple of Jerusalem, but generally it doesn't seem that the Pharisees themselves became the Rabbis who wrote down the oral teachings in the Talmud. For one thing, the Mishnah[37] and a commentary on it was written in the Land of Israel before the Babylonian Talmud was written. The Talmud we know today was written in what we now call Iraq from 300–600 CE. So most of the scholars who ended up having an influence on Rabbinic Judaism were in Iraq (Babylonia), and Rabbinic Judaism was still taking form in the 2nd and 3rd century, just as the Jesus Movement was morphing into Christianity, so there was no clear authority or power center in either Jewish or Christian groups at this time.

We do know that in the second century CE, in contrast to the Christians, who still considered The Book of Enoch important, the Sages (the rabbis who wrote the Talmud) started to reject the interpretation of Gen 6:1-4 that appears in Enoch. In fact, neither the Mishnah, Tosefta,[38] Jerusalem Talmud, Babylonian Talmud, nor any midrashic[39] compilations contain any references to Enochian texts at all. The power of the Sages grew, however, at the same time as the Christianization of the Roman Empire spread. Despite all this attention to the Law that is crystalized in the form of the Talmud, however, the practice of magic both among the Rabbis and ordinary Jews increased.

The Midrash values a multiplicity of voices and very much prizes the interaction of views even in the Torah, but there is no inclusion of the very different perspective of Enoch as a possible interpretation of Gen 6:1-4. Perhaps a reason for this is that Enoch does not foreground interpretations of the Halakhah in the Hebrew Bible, and that was the focus of Rabbinic Judaism. Only later does an alternative interpretation of Gen 6:1–4 appear, in Genesis Rabbah[40] 26:5–7.

In that book, we learn the following: Shimon bar Yochai interpreted "the sons of Elohim saw" (Genesis 6:2) as "judges" and curses anyone who says they are sons of the Divine or of divine entities. He also taught that sexuality that violates Halakhah is only sinful when powerful people engage in it, an interesting take. In that case, we could focus on the powerful "people" who were the Watchers or on the human women, who were not powerful; either perspective would change how we interpret the Watchers story and how it relates to evil. He does question why in the text it says "sons of divine beings." The miracle worker Hanina ben Dosa and Shimon ben Lakish both said that the Watchers were called "sons of Elohim" because they lived to be very old without getting sick or being punished in any way (which of course demonstrates that these two Sages did not know Enoch).

Rabbah bar bar Hana[41] said that they were called "sons of Elohim" because they were in charge of the seasons and astronomy. They and their progeny would be punished. This sounds like he is describing the Watchers from Enoch. Yudan said that "they took wives from those who pleased them" from Gen 6:2 means that at that time the most powerful man of the town would take virgin brides first, before the groom, and would also take women who were beautiful even if they were already married to someone else as well as men and animals if they wanted. Rav Huna[42] says that God determined to send the destructive Flood only when people wrote marriage contracts between people and animals.

This is a great example of how it is typical for all sorts of views to interact on a page of the Talmud. Notice that not one single view is pronounced to be correct. It's like the conversation is still going on. And indeed, commentary is still the basis of how Halakhah is interpreted today in Judaism. The reality of how different views coexist in religious texts is very different from how some people elect to condemn "Abrahamic" religions as monologic—putting forward only one view and enforcing its acceptance.

Enoch and the Canon in Judaism

However, people who read Rabbinic literature did conclude that the "sons of Elohim" were not angels but human beings. At the time, some sects considered it heretical (I think the issue was whether angels could sin or have sex) and viewed it as a threat to Rabbinic authority, which was still shaky. In Rabbinics, it was prevalent to view angels as inferior to human beings and so, like animals, they could not sin. Humans were given the Torah specifically because they *can* sin; Halakhah is not for angels. This has a weird resonance later when Christians begin to condemn Jews precisely for having Halakhah, claiming that Jews were naturally evil and needed a lot of strict laws. This also contradicts the views of most Jews before Rabbinism. People like Enoch and Noah are seen to be either almost angelic or literally as having been transformed into angels, which was viewed as an ascent, not a downgrade.

The fragments of Enoch found at Qumran were, at the latest, from the first century BCE; since we see no further Jewish copies of Enoch until the Middle Ages, when it is mentioned in the Zohar along with The Book of Adam, both of which the Zohar describes as ancient magic books. We don't even find any excerpts or quotations from it in Judaism. The only mentions of Enoch at all were to the effect that he had not been raised to Heaven. The first mention at all of Enoch was not until 600 CE. We hear nothing about any descent of angels until after the Talmud is finished; then it is again treated in 3 Enoch (see section on 3 Enoch), *Pirqe de Rabbi Eliezer*,[43] and mentioned in Pesiqta Rabbati, medieval midrashic writings like Aggadat Bereshit, Bereshit Rabbati, and Yalqut Shimoni, and the Zohar and Rashi. Note that these mentions refer to the descent of the angels as described in Enoch, not the Christian story of the Battle in Heaven and the Fall of the Angels, which does not appear in any Jewish texts.

When Jewish texts after the rise of Rabbinism do begin to mention the story of the angels' descent, instead of focusing on the angels' sexual desire for women, they zero in on what the angels taught and how that affected people and the Earth in general. It seems to me that the focus shifts because the category of what an angel can do shifts; if they are not human and Halakhah is not for them, they can't sin in that way and instead do something for which there is no law—sharing knowledge. However, we could point out—and some did—that there is no commandment forbidding angels from having sex with humans either. Although some people have argued (and still do) that The Book of Enoch was suppressed or that the story of Enoch becoming an angel was smashed, there is no proof of that. It just didn't fit with the dominant view of the universal order in Rabbinism.

Why did The Book of Enoch become a topic of interest among certain Jews after Rabbinism, in the Middle Ages? Precisely because of the rise of the work of Merkavah mysticism, in which the spirit, mind, soul, or intact body of an individual could learn how to ascend to Heaven and view the throne of God in person, similar to what Enoch accomplished.

Gershom Scholem believed that the Watchers story was connected to the source of Merkavah mysticism and that we didn't have any historical proof of that because the story was passed down orally and secretly; it was esoteric knowledge. He also believed that there were connections between the apocalyptic writings of Second Temple Judaism and Hekhalot, which not only involves rising through the seven heavens but also incorporates magical practices like adjuring angels to appear before the magic worker in order that various boons be granted, especially knowledge of the Torah and a solid memory (which would allow the magic worker to become the go-to individual in their community for making rulings on various questions, on the same level as a rabbi). There is no historical evidence for this connection either, but again, he thought it was passed on secretly. The problem with things being passed on secretly is that there is no proof of their existence, much less tracing their origins or how they affect people.

Rabbi Moshe ha-Darshan's book, *Bereshit Rabbati*,[44] written in the 11th century, was preserved in extract form in a 13th-century text *(Pugio Fidei)* used by a Dominican to try to convert Jews and Muslims to Christianity. *Bereshit Rabbati* has not been found as a stand-alone text but combined into other manuscripts. It contains the Watchers story, but sticks to two angels, Shemihazah and Asael. They decide to have a contest about who can resist evil longer. They think that they will be able to do that much longer than mere humans are able to, but instead, they end up "cavorting with the daughters of men."

There's an interesting version of this story in which Shemihazah tries to seduce a woman named Asterah (this name means "star," which seems related to her fate but also has resonance with the Watchers as stars). She tells him she will give in to him if he teaches her which Divine Name he uses to ascend to the first Heaven. He teaches her, and she craftily uses it to ascend to Heaven, leaving him in the dust. God turns her into the Pleiades. It's interesting that a human woman is turned into stars, which we will see is what the Watchers were in charge of; in this way she trumps him twice, by tricking him and then by being raised to do one of the tasks the Watchers screwed up and abandoned, proving she is more steadfast and smarter than they are. Further, she is able to rise bodily to Heaven just as Enoch, a favored man, did, and to gain immortality as—true, not an angel, but close—as a group of stars. In most Hekhalot literature, which is all about rising to Heaven and making one's way through its Palaces, the person who is able to do this feat of mystical and magical power is a man. However, the rejection of sexual activity as part of the purification necessary to prepare for ascent is also modeled with her.

One scholar has said "magical power grows out of sexuality," but it is perhaps better to say it grows out of the cessation of it. On the other hand, it is because of sexuality that the angel approaches her in the first place. Both active sexuality and its rejection seem to provide a motor for magical action in Hekhalot stories.

The other interesting aspect of this story is the involvement of trickery to gain favor. One of the most striking motifs in Genesis is how important trickery and the reversal of (mis)fortune are in the stories.

CHAPTER SIX

Enoch in Early Christianity

Jewish Christianity had come into existence by the 2nd to the 3rd centuries CE, but not all Christian groups grew out of Judaism, especially as time went by. We know that early followers of Jesus knew of The Watchers and that it was referred to in the Book of Jude (which has a major role in the Christian perspective on The Watchers), 1 Peter, and 2 Peter, which are among the earliest Christian scriptures.

One thing that stands out about this period is that neither Jewish nor Christian writings were critiquing what the angels taught; they ignored that issue, which came to be important only later, after the Adam and Eve story ended up dominating the explanation of the origin of evil. Instead, for the most part, both Jews and Christians zeroed in on the Watchers' sexual offenses. They basically rejected the idea that evil came from Heaven and caused human suffering and the spread of sin through the Watchers' teachings.

Early Christians found value in Jewish scriptures—like Enoch—that were making the rounds of Jews who were not part of the move to Rabbinism. Christians collected and edited these texts and wrote new ones under the name of ancient figures from the Hebrew Bible. They also composed texts under the names of the apostles and eventually created works by early Church leaders ("Church Fathers") who wrote Greco-Roman texts under their own name.

Early Christian leaders who interpreted the Hebrew Bible in the 2nd and 3rd centuries saw the "sons of Elohim" of Gen 6:1–4 as angels, rather than deeming them human or the sons of Cain, views which evolved later. Seeing these figures as angels was not considered to be heretical or a fringe view at that time, even though later that would be the case.

A major Christian writer who addressed the contents of Enoch was Justin Martyr (100–165 CE), an early Church writer who adapted Greek philosophy to Christianity. He said that the angels corrupted human beings, and he is among the first to assert that the angels' teachings spread evil on Earth. He believed that the Watchers turned divine revelation upside-down in their teachings, which basically enslaved and corrupted human beings instead of liberating them. According to him, the Watchers gave humans magic books and taught them to worship the Watchers with sacrifices, libations, and incense. He also says that the Watchers were responsible for causing adultery, recklessness, murder, and other varieties of evil, which is similar to what is described in Enoch itself. He doesn't even mention Adam and Eve. However, he does extend his condemnation of the Watchers to contemporary Jews. In his mind, both the Watchers and Jews deliberately reject God (particularly in the form of Jesus) and that both, having become corrupt, go on to corrupt others. He contrasts Jews to Pagans, who to his mind are just led astray by the Watchers (although in Enoch it is much more the role of the spirits of the Nephilim who are responsible for the turning of humans to the worship of idols). He is considered an originator of Jew-hatred in Christianity.

In *Dialog with Trypho* (155–160 CE), which is a fictional description of a Christian and Jew debating the validity of their respective religions, Justin asserts that death came about because of the events that occurred in the Garden of Eden. The story of Enoch and the Watchers recedes from importance in Christianity as the characters of Adam, Eve, and the Serpent begin to take over the description of how evil arose on Earth, especially once Augustine created the concept of original sin.

Christians found a number of reasons to preserve Enoch. Irenaeus of Lyons (130–200 CE), a Greek bishop best known for doing his best to keep Gnosticism out of Christianity, pointed out that Enoch, who existed prior even to Abraham, was therefore uncircumcised and yet he was lifted up to Heaven to sit next to the divine throne and to be immortal. To Christians, this functioned as proof that Christians were not obligated to even observe the Sabbath; they could ignore it and still be saved. This meant that pretty much everything in the Torah was superfluous, which was a huge advantage to Christians. They would no longer have to be dependent on Judaism in the sense of observing Halakhah, they could attract more people to Christianity and not have to confine their recruiting efforts to Jews, and they could cast Judaism and its pesky Halakhah in the outmoded category—the Old Covenant with its "Old Testament."

They even came to see Halakhah not as a divine gift but as a punishment. Justin Martyr wrote that Halakhah was given to Jews because they were "hard-hearted." It was as if God knew all along that Jews would reject Jesus as a divine messiah, so God punished Jews in advance of that rejection by giving them innumerable obnoxious commandments to carry out that would regulate a huge amount of everyday life. As far as Christians were concerned, because Jews had rejected Jesus as the divine Messiah, the Temple of Jerusalem was destroyed, and Jews were expelled from the city.

Some Christians came to see Enoch as a prophetic text. Information in the book about the Messiah was seen by some as a foreshadowing of the life of Christ and a prediction of subsequent church teachings. Enoch was viewed by some Christians as a pre-Christian witness and validation of Christianity. Church figures like Tertullian[45] saw Enoch as sacred scripture that was inspired by the Holy Spirit. However, although most Christians did find Enoch to be a type of pre-Christian verification of Christianity and valued it enough to make copies of it, they didn't consider it to be divinely inspired.

Christian Attitudes About the Angels' Teachings

One major difference between the Jewish and Christian uses of The Book of Enoch was that Christians began to focus on the effect of the Watchers' teachings rather than on the actions of the angels in coming to earth. This was a new development. Previous to Justin Martyr, Christians saw the problem in the Watchers story as the angels' actions with women instead of their teachings. A century later, Cyprian[46] was claiming that the Watchers' teaching must have been bad because of their actions, which showed the angels to have been the problem. Because of what the angels did, whatever they might have taught would have been corrupted and corrupting. The Watchers' teachings came to be foregrounded specifically in the Christian approach to Enoch.

Eventually, Christians came to consider that the Watchers sinned by transmitting teachings that corrupted human beings as well as revealing secrets that human beings were never meant to know.

Demons, Hell, and Satan

Asael, one of the leaders of the Watchers, was punished by being incarcerated, surrounded by sharp rocks, in a black space beneath the ground. Although there are a few mentions of a fiery hell for the Watchers who sinned in Enoch (basically where the Watchers would go at the end of time), Christians created a different vision of Hell. For them, beginning with Irenaeus of Lyons, Hell was a place where not only the Watchers would burn forever but likewise every human who was not righteous, who was wicked, godless, and profane.

Having created this version of Hell, Christians designated someone to be master of it—Satan. There is no Satan in Judaism, so the assertion that Judaism was dualistic with good and evil at the beginning is not correct. In fact, in Judaism, it is generally said that God created both. Demons (who were generally nameless) could attack and possess people, and the earliest Jewish magic we have found is exorcism of demons from people. But Judaism has never had a devil-in-chief like Satan and so there was no one to lead any battle against God in Heaven.

For Christians, demons became more and more active in the world and basically grew to be an infestation from whom no one was safe. Justin Martyr had already argued that Pagans were convinced by demons to worship them (in the form of Pagan gods). Demons also caused Pagans to persecute Christians, and demons likewise attacked Christians to make them become heretics. As the perceived threat of Christian heresy grew, Satan was brought up more and more.

While the popularity of Enoch among Christians was at first motivated by its use as a proof that Halakhah was not important for Christians and that it foretold Jesus as the Messiah, we can also see that as the interest in demons increased, so did Christian attentions given to Enoch, which "explains" how demons arrived as the hybrid children of misbehaving angels and women, and how 10 percent of the souls of the Nephilim were allowed to survive the Flood in order to bedevil human beings until the day came that God ended the world. Demons swarmed like vermin in the Christian view and empowered Jews' rejection of Jesus and Roman persecution of Christians.

In effect, many aspects of the Watchers' story were transferred to Satan and were not connected to the interpretation of Genesis 6:1–4 anymore. For Christians, especially with Augustine, Satan became way worse than any Watchers could ever be, especially because in the Christian rendering, Satan was still present and commanding growing armies of demons, whereas the Watchers were a puny group of two hundred or so and were locked up in black spaces beneath sharp rocks, unable to do anything. Not only was Satan mentioned in Christian Scriptures but since Paul referred to Jesus as the new Adam, Christians came to zero in on the story of Adam and Eve and leave the Watchers, the Flood, and Enoch behind.

Enoch in Christian Scripture: The Example of Mark

The story of the Gerasene demoniac is a good illustration of the new Christian focus on demons. This story occurs in three Gospels, the earliest mention being in Mark 5:1–20. This is the tale of how a man was possessed by a legion of demons; Jesus threw them out and put them into a herd of pigs, which then ran down into a lake and drowned. This story has clear markings of a relationship to Enoch, which carried a lot of mythic weight among Christians even when it was not considered to be divinely inspired.

Some of the elements of the story of this exorcism resonate with *The Watchers*. For instance, the man who is possessed has some features in common with the Nephilim—he might not be a giant, but he is enormously strong and can break any chains put on him. Also, the demon who is infesting the victim resides in the hole dug into the mountains among the tombs. We can say that since demons were created on Earth, it's natural for them to reside in the earth, but this also coincides with the prison of the Watchers—a black space beneath the surface of the Earth. The demon in Mark cut himself with sharp rocks, which in some ways goes to verify his insane strength but in others refers to the sharp rocks Archangel Raphael uses to cover the Watcher Asael in the dark place in which he is imprisoned until the end of time. The demons possessing the man are thrown into a large herd of pigs that drown themselves in the water, just as the vast majority of the Nephilim would be drowned in the Flood.

There is another interesting connection, however—how the demon addresses Jesus. He uses the Greek translation of "son of the Most High." This same phrase is used in the Greek translation of Enoch as a replacement for YHVH, the Hebrew personal name of the Divine.

Enoch and the Christian Canon

In the third century CE, Christians began wondering why Enoch had not been included in the Jewish canon. They could not understand why Jews didn't think the book was authoritative. Christians still had not created their own canon, but by this time they did consider Enoch to be Scripture.

"Hard-hearted" as they might be, Jews, especially learned ones who lived in the Land of Israel, were esteemed by Christians as experts on the Hebrew Bible. Christians argued that if Jews doubted Enoch, then maybe there was something wrong with it and Christians should doubt it too.

At the same time, many Christians saw Jews as a direct challenge to the Church's authority and especially to Christianity's appropriation of the Hebrew Bible and other sacred Jewish texts, which Christians considered gave authenticity to Christianity in terms of an ancientness that Christianity did not possess. Re-reading ancient Jewish texts like Enoch as precursors and foretellers of Christianity—as if they had been written by Christians or that their authors embedded secret messages in the text that foretold Christianity—was an important part of that authentication, but if the text they were using for that purpose turned out to be considered inauthentic by learned Jews, then Christians were almost duty-bound to reject it.

Tertullian believed that Enoch was in fact divinely inspired because it contained Christian ideas, and if a text was divinely inspired, then it was "suitable for edification," according to Timothy 3:16. He argued that Jews were rejecting the authenticity of Enoch precisely because it foretold Jesus and worked as proof that one didn't have to obey Halakhah in order to be loved by God and even be lifted up to Heaven. Tertullian also wasn't so sure how trustworthy Jews were with respect to ancient texts.

In contrast, Origen believed Jews were the ultimate authority on ancient Jewish texts and even studied Hebrew to become more knowledgeable about these texts.

Athanasius of Alexandria (296–373 CE) claimed that The Book of Enoch was written by a heretic; he conveniently ignored the fact that it is quoted in Jude, where we are told that Enoch prophesied how God would bring legions of angels to punish sinners.

Augustine of Hippo[47] wrote that the Jewish canon didn't include The Book of Enoch because Jews didn't consider its claims to ancientness to be authentic. To him, this was a good reason for Christians to doubt its authenticity too.

That The Book of Enoch was not in the Jewish canon was a good reason for Christians to reject it, but it wasn't the only one. There was another obstacle to the book becoming more accepted among Christians which was not ideological; there was no Latin translation of it. Church leaders who had written about it had used the Greek translation, but Latin was quickly becoming the international language of the Christians of the Roman and Byzantine Empires. It was when in 380 CE that Christianity became the imperial religion of the Roman Empire, in which Latin was the international language, that Christians rejected Enoch. Oddly enough, although they had rejected Enochic literature and Christianity was triumphal, in the 4th and 5th centuries Christians still were concerned about what Jews thought was authentic. Also, many Christians still engaged in Jewish rituals and practices.

It was only when Christian leaders began to put together the Christian canon that they rejected the story of the Watchers and Enochic literature altogether.

CHAPTER SEVEN

The Evolution of the Watchers

Both Christians and Jews came to consider the "sons of God" not to be angels but instead concluded that they were actually human beings, usually of some socially exalted type (thus, they were social "giants"). The Aramaic versions of the Hebrew Bible go so far as to translate the phrase *bnei Elohim* as "sons of Judges" or "sons of nobles." If instead of angels they were simply men, we need an explanation of why they received a punishment as dire as the destruction of the world for simply taking women as wives, which is not forbidden. One such explanation comes in Genesis Rabbah 26:5, where it was written that these men were nobles and chieftains; they gave themselves the right of the first night with new brides (which would be adultery), but also engaged in pedophilia and bestiality, about which they even composed music (so celebrating it rather than doing this in some furtive way). They had no shame about engaging in these sins.

The Sons of Seth and the Daughters of Cain

An alternative explanation for this event was created by Julius Africanus (160–240 CE), who was born in Jerusalem and knew Greek, Latin, and Hebrew. He was a Pagan who became a Christian. He composed a number of historical texts, which influenced early Christian leaders. In his opinion, no angels were described in Genesis 6:1–4. Instead, the reference was to the sons of Seth, the son of Adam and Eve. Seth was born after the death of Abel and the exile of Cain. He was the ancestor of Noah, and so the sons of Seth were descended from the non-evil, "godly" line of Adam and Eve. As such, they should have married women descended from the Seth line, as well, but instead, they chose women from among Cain's descendants. These "daughters of Cain" taught the "sons of Seth" evil things, such as reading the stars for magical purposes and worshiping idols. By the fifth century, this explanation for the "sons of God" pushed aside the story of angels.

The sons of Seth explanation might have come into Judaism from Christianity. It's not mentioned until the early Middle Ages in the *Pirqe de Rabbi Eliezer*.

Another reason why Christians might have abandoned the idea of the "sons of God" being angels is that Julius Africanus was made fun of by well-known Pagan writers like Emperor Julian (331–363 CE), the last Pagan Roman emperor who fought to revive ancient Roman religion, and Celsus, who lived during the second century CE and was known for being anti-Christian in his writings. Justin Martyr quoted Celsus, who strongly held that ancient Roman and Greek religion was against the kind of super-stition that he considered a major part of Christianity. Both Celsus and the Emperor Julian specifically targeted the idea of the virgin birth and the Christian concept of Jesus having existed from the beginning of time (the Incarnation).

The other motive is that the Adam and Eve story rose in importance just as the story of the Watchers was morphed into Christianity's story of the battle in Heaven led by Satan, who didn't come down to Earth just before the Flood, like the Watchers, but who had existed since the begin-ning of the Creation, an odd resonance with the Incarnation idea.

One thing is clear: *Christians didn't outlaw or suppress Enoch.* This is important for us to remember, because many claim nowadays that the Church deliberately hid Enoch in order to conceal something. Histori-cally, this isn't true. The fact is that Enoch just wasn't important to them anymore. They had other stories that they liked more and that made more sense to them as their own mythology grew. Enoch quit fitting into that mythology. Because it wasn't being read anymore, it didn't continue to be copied, and so, over the centuries, it became lost. In the West, it survived only in fragments of the Greek translation that were made in the 5th and 6th centuries.

The fact that this text was so marginalized might be one of the reasons why some people gave it more status and value than it might have otherwise received. This was true for the Coptic Egyptians of the early part of the first millennium as well as it is now. The Watchers story became important in Hermetic groups. In many ways, the teachings of the Watchers are a pretty close match to the alchemical ways of working with dyes, coloring of and working with metals, use of constellations to make magic, and so forth. In fact, the first time I read about the Watchers' teachings, I thought immediately of alchemy.

Structure of Enoch

When R.H. Charles[18] translated Enoch from the Ethiopic version, he put forward the idea that Enoch was composed of at least five books. This conclusion has stood since then. At the time, of course printing did not exist; books were written by hand on (usually leather) scrolls. Other Enochic works from the 2nd century BCE share the same traditions as Enoch and were often bound together with Enoch in the manuscripts from Qumran and the Ethiopic compilation known as Enoch.

The Book of The Watchers

The one book within Enoch that has had the most influence on Western culture is The Watchers, which is in turn composed of multiple texts written by more than one person. The fact that it has multiple authors is one of the reasons why it's polysemic—in other words, multiple meanings are part of its nature. That is why there is not one single meaning for anything in Enoch, only meaning possibilities that slide into and past each other like the multiple possible meanings of dreams. We hear a lot of talk from people who are certain that sacred texts speak with one dominating voice and who act like they've won a prize when they find contradictions and different stories for the same thing in a sacred text, but the fact is that sacred texts are generally self-contradictory for many reasons, not least of which being that not one single person wrote them or used them.

The most important part of The Watchers resides in chapters 6–11. This is often seen as a kind of midrash or expansion/explanation of Genesis 6:1–4, but some scholars believe that it is older than Genesis and even that this story goes all the way back to the time of the First Temple (1000 BCE). This makes sense to me because it is so profoundly different from what has since been accepted as the origin of sin (the Adam and Eve story); it has that alien ring that we sometimes get from ancient things. Also, you will see later that the oldest versions of this story are the least misogynistic. It does seem that in this neck of the woods, the ancients accorded more of a place for women, which lessened with the centuries.

The Watchers story is vitally important to Enoch in terms of showing us how some people came to conceptualize good and evil and where it came from/how it arose, the appearance and persistence of demons, and the dangers of forbidden knowledge.

Even though The Watchers is the most important book in Enoch, it is not about Enoch. Instead, it is about Shemihazah and Asael, two Watchers who led a group of 200 other angels from Heaven to earth to find wives among women. The story of either angel seems to have existed independently in the distant past and was combined in order to create The Watchers. Some consider that the Shemihazah story came first, and others that the Asael story is older. The fact that these two different stories about the angels' descent exist side by side in The Watchers shows that people were not finished with interpreting this event yet. I think that this is also a good example of how an ancient text can tolerate contradictions in ways that would not be acceptable in modern texts of various kinds. It's as if the ancients were not only fine with the rough edges but in some way appreciated them—certainly enough not to try to eradicate or silence them. Also, the contradictory stories are not left there by accident or because the ancients didn't have the sense or skill to homogenize the stories; they wanted them there.

The two angels, Shemihazah and Asael, had different motivations:

Shemihazah had the idea of going down to Earth to have sex with women and then asked the other Watchers to swear they went with him freely so that he alone would not be blamed for doing that. Women were basically Shemihazah's targeted victims.

In contrast, the angel Asael brought forbidden knowledge down to Earth, where humans were eager to adopt this knowledge. At a certain point, we can't tell whether the knowledge was forbidden to the Watchers, whether it was forbidden to share with humans, or whether it was a matter of forbidden topics. I will take that up later.

One thing we notice right away is that the story of the Watchers is told like an ordinary third-person narration. It's not Enoch who is telling the story in the first person, as in many other parts of Enoch.

There is a short introduction by Enoch about how God will soon manifest on Earth with vast hosts (this is the version of God who is Lord of Hosts). Mountains will shake, break apart, and fall; the ground will be torn apart, the living will die, and the angels will tremble. This will be a day of judgment, when God will save the righteous and destroy the wicked. This vision of apocalypse serves as a backdrop for the entire book. It defines the book as being focused on where sin came from, what it is, how it affects people and the Earth, and what will happen as a result—a sorting out of the righteous and the wrongdoers.

Enoch encourages his readers to look to natural objects as an inspiration to righteousness. Stars follow their divinely ordained courses and can be counted upon to appear when they are expected to. The seasons come according to their time. The plants change in a regular cycle and predictable pattern; trees shed their leaves in winter and plants bloom in spring. All this is according to divine command. There is a strong focus on order. Obviously, we are told that to be righteous, we must follow the path that God has set out for us and follow the commandments.

The Evolution of the Watchers

Next comes the story of the Watchers. In chapters 6–11, there are three different descriptions of what the Watchers do wrong. The section that most closely follows Genesis 6:1–4 is chapters 6–7. The Watchers looked down to Earth, saw women, and wanted them for wives but also, something that is not often mentioned, they wanted them to give them children. After Shemihazah voices his concern that he will be blamed for getting the other angels to go down to Earth, the others all swear that they voluntarily went with him. Two hundred of them go down to Earth. We are then given a list of the names of the twenty chiefs of these angels, each in charge of their own group of ten.

They choose the women they want and have sex with them and "defile themselves" with the women. It's not clear what "defile" means, but at this point it seems they are defiling themselves because angels have no business having sex at all, much less with women, which is a transgression in the sense of crossing the boundary between two species, combining things that should be kept separate, an important concept in Judaism. The Watchers teach the women sorcery, charms, and the cutting of roots and plants in general. This is the first description of "forbidden knowledge" we get in the book.

The women bear giants, known as the Nephilim, who eat all the things that belonged to human beings. Once they are done with that, they start eating people. They also have sex with birds, mammals, reptiles, and fish, and drink each other's blood. The earth cries out against them.

Asael taught people how to make weapons of war from metal—swords, knives, shields, coats of mail—as well as how to make bracelets and ornaments, how to use antimony to shadow their eyes, how to make their eyebrows beautiful, create gems, and make coloring tinctures. This caused everyone to have sex with each other, to become generally corrupt, and to forget about God. We then get a curriculum of each angel's forbidden arts.

As a result of the angels' actions, a lot of people died, crying out to God as they did so. The world was very much changed from what it had been before the Watchers arrived. The souls of the dead cried to Heaven for justice.

Four archangels heard their cries and confronted God about the situation. Why had God done nothing even though God must have foreseen these events?

God decided to destroy the Earth by flood, and sent the archangel Sariel (aka Uriel) to tell Noah that he should hide himself and prepare because a great flood was going to occur. God told Raphael to bind Asael, put him in a dark space in the desert, pile sharp rocks on him, and cover his face (as is done with the dead); on the day of judgment, he would be thrown into the great fire.

God said that the earth would be healed from the destruction brought upon it by the actions of the Nephilim and the teachings of the Watchers, in particular Asael's teachings. Gabriel said that God ought to destroy all the children of the Watchers by sending them out to battle to kill each other, even though they originally were meant to live for five hundred years, and no matter how their fathers ask for mercy for their children, they should not get it. God tells Michael to bind Shemihazah and all the other angels who had been involved in this event. After they have seen all their children destroyed, they would remain bound in the valleys of the earth for seventy generations. At the end of time, they would be tortured forever. Even the spirits of their children would be destroyed. When this is over, God says the earth will bloom abundantly and peace will reign.

In the next section, Enoch appears and is taken up to Heaven. The Watchers give him a petition for God's mercy, and Enoch ascends to Heaven to present it to God. God refuses to show them any mercy. Enoch next sees the underworld and the place where the angels will be punished, and he learns the secrets of weather. He is told the names of the archangels and what they do.

On a second journey he is shown Sheol,[48] the Underworld, and faraway places on Earth, with a special focus on local weather and astronomy.

The different versions of the story of the Watchers have the same conclusion. The Nephilim committed great violence against the earth and its creatures. The earth or human beings cried out to Heaven. In each version we find sexual offenses, the transmission of forbidden and corrupting knowledge, and the violence committed by the Watchers' children, which leads to the Flood.

Even though Enoch was obviously important to the people of Qumran—they made multiple copies of it—they didn't refer to the story of the Watchers in most of the texts they themselves wrote.

The Watchers and Inconsistency in Enoch

Enoch features three versions of the Watchers story: 6–19; 67:6, 69; and 86-88. These versions differ but have certain features in common. We might think that Enoch is inconsistent precisely because it's non-canonical and so hasn't been combed through to make it as consistent as one might think that canonical texts like the Pentateuch are. But there are massively inconsistent parts of that sacred text, beginning with Genesis, where we get two contradictory views of how human beings were created. As mentioned above, God creates Adam from clay and then removes his rib while he is asleep. God forms the first woman from that rib. This is the version most of us have heard. But an earlier version tells us that God created both male and female from clay at the same time. Personally, I like that version better, and I especially like that the text itself offers us a choice; it's only centuries later that we are told outside of the text that one version is truth.

The way many modern readers of these sorts of canonical inconsistencies read them is simply to choose one version as important or correct and either just not mention the other or claim that it's metaphorical. But the ancients generally had a different attitude.

In some ways, ancient minds were much more flexible than modern ones, but also, in ancient texts contradictory versions of events are presented to perhaps give full voice to the community that wrote the text (the scribes and different groups among them). The tendency to add on rather than remove (although there are removals in canonical texts, like the bulk of Miriam's Song of the Sea in Exodus and even Miriam's importance as a leader and prophet altogether). But adding on is also a way to give full voice to the community that hears the text. Remember that this book was not typically read privately by a single person. For one thing, many people were not literate and making books (hand copying scrolls) was expensive, so instead, texts were typically read aloud to a group, and that group had the right to talk back to it and discuss it. More than one scholar has suggested that these readings involved a back and forth between the person reading it aloud and those listening, a kind of call and response at the very least (so for instance at the most important works for a particular group), which is more likely to allow for argument and discussion.

This kind of reading fits right in with how even canonical texts were traditionally received in ancient Jewish culture—such that there was an obligation for members of the public to come and hear the Torah read publicly once a week. One of the aspects of this public reading now is that at least one other person follows the written text to make sure that it is read correctly by the reader, but anyone sitting in the congregation can pipe up with the correction, in fact.

There is also the long tradition in Judaism of studying a text by arguing about it aloud with a partner or in a group. I haven't found any mention of how long this tradition goes back, but we know from the Talmud that this type of reception was usual as long ago as the first century CE.

Enoch is an ancient text, which means it might not be (and is not) at all internally consistent and is not bothered by that fact. But remember that it's composed of at least five different books that were themselves written separately by different scribes in various places and times and then put together. Even if we were to read the first part of Enoch as condemning women for at the very least helping to corrupt the world after the Watchers taught them skills like casting spells and divination—specifically, for instance, seen as Babylonian evils—later in the book we find the wives are not at all blamed for the corruption of the world. In fact, in a recounting of what happened, the Watchers don't even teach humans any such skills, nor are women responsible for "enticing" the angels from Heaven.

The further we move forward in time, the more likely are interpretations to blame women for practicing the magic the angels teach and for promoting licentiousness thanks to the makeup and jewelry humans learn how to make because of Asael's teaching, but some of the later Greek translations and the excerpts from it even modify the original text to ensure that women are to blame. So, remarkably enough, the ancients were nowhere near as misogynist as more modern cultures, at least in Enoch.

We can put forward that Enoch might be transmitting traditions outside of the Hebrew Bible. There is no reason to think that Judaism was a homogeneous monolith in ancient times (or later, for that matter). Just with respect to Enoch, consider, for instance, that in the Hebrew Bible, the Flood is not the result of the actions of the Watchers (see Gen:6-8). What's more, there is no Biblical commandment against the Watchers having sex with human beings.

The core of The Watchers is chapters 6–11, and that section can be said to have nothing to do with any Enochic tradition, because Enoch is not even mentioned in it. Instead, that part is all about the Watchers and their fall. Enoch doesn't turn up until chapters 12:1–2, and it seems tacked on.

An interesting aspect of The Watchers is the location of some of its action—Tel Dan in upper Galilee. This place is right near the Hermon Mountains, which is where the Watchers were said to have descended from Heaven. The area has been the site of ancient Israelite sacred sites dating back to the Middle Bronze Age (2100–1550 BCE). Two golden calves were placed by Jeroboam, one in Dan and the other in Bethel, the place where Jacob had his dream of the ladder to Heaven, and which is also said to be near where Abraham placed his tent and welcomed the angels.

It's interesting that the setting of a text that tells of a human being going up to and coming down from Heaven is linked to a place where a Patriarch dreamed of precisely that kind of movement, and also that this going up and down by angels partly foretells what will become of Enoch.

Golden calf worship was an ancient part of Israelite religion, but it was criticized as being too much like idolatry. Jeroboam didn't want people of the two tribes he ruled going on pilgrimages to Jerusalem, which everyone was supposed to do at certain times for ritual purposes. The two golden calves were meant to provide a throne for God to sit on, just as God was said to sit above the angels depicted on the Ark of the Covenant.

It was at Tel Dan that the Watchers sat down. We can conclude that setting Tel Dan as the location of the Watchers is a way of reinforcing the idea of their rebelliousness.

It's pretty clear that The Watchers came from two different sources, but the two stories can't be teased apart anymore. It does not look like it was actually written to explain the bit of Genesis that mentions the Watchers, nor is its purpose to stand in lieu of the Torah. It stands on its own, part of a different sacred endeavor.

Similitudes

The next book in Enoch is Similitudes. Our version was translated into Ethiopic from Aramaic and is often thought to have been written during the period of Herod the Great (72 BCE–4 BCE), which makes it very late—the most recently written of the five books in Enoch. It was composed in the last part of the first century BCE or the beginning of the first century CE. However, even though it was supposedly composed during Herod the Great's refurbishing of the Temple of Jerusalem, this book doesn't mention that. What's more, although Aramaic fragments of the rest of Enoch have been found at Qumran and prove its origin in the ancient Holy Land, no fragments of Similitudes have ever been found in any Semitic language; it has not even been found in a Greek translation, only in Ethiopic. This has led some scholars to assert that this part of Enoch wasn't written until the middle of the first century CE or even later.

Although this book is also called The Book of Parables, it is composed not of parables as we know them from the Gospels, a symbol-filled story, but is instead made up of revelations. So already we see a couple of problems with how this book does or doesn't fit into Enoch as a whole. But there's more.

Some say that Similitudes was written late enough to be a Christian text, and certainly Christians read the "Son of Man" mentioned in the

The Evolution of the Watchers

book as designating Jesus, but the book itself identifies that figure with Enoch, so we can't really say it's a Christian-originated work on that basis.

In chapter 52 of Similitudes, we are told about six mountains, which are composed of metals. This is an example of the kind of metallurgical knowledge which, on the one hand, was given to humans by Asael and condemned as forbidden but also is clearly okay at this point in the text, because it's knowledge that an angel that hasn't disobeyed the divine order shares with Enoch. Personally, to me it is strange that there are not seven mountains and seven metals, since seven is such an important number not only for the Israelites but for many other ancient peoples (due to the number of planets visible to the human eye). This makes me wonder if a line got chopped from Similitudes by accident.

In Similitudes, it's not Heaven that is described but who Enoch sees there—namely, God as "The Lord of Spirits." And although Enoch sees the throne of God in this book, there's a contradiction between the description of the figures supporting the heavenly throne in Similitudes and how they appear in Ezekiel's vision, which is the original source (as far as we know). In Ezekiel's version, four sacred creatures support the throne and are referred to as Cherubim. This name is used for sacred creatures in other cultures of the general region as well, but in Judaism, Cherubim have the bodies of men instead of being chimeric, and they are definitely not little babies with wings, as they are often depicted in Classical paintings or modern material culture. We are told that they have four faces: a man, a lion, an ox, and an eagle. These angels support the throne and are different in appearance from those who sleep not—the Watchers. They are named Michael, who is merciful and patient; Raphael, who cures disease and heals wounds; Gabriel, who commands all powers; and Phanuel, who oversees the hope that comes from repentance.

Although the archangels around the throne are depicted, Heaven itself is not described in this section. But there is another figure there, separate from God, who is called the Righteous One, the Chosen One, the Anointed One, and the Son of Man. This individual looks like a human being, but his face is full of graciousness, as if he were an angel. In the future, this figure will fight for righteous people chosen for their godliness and piety, and he will condemn kings and powerful people who have oppressed them. It is clear from the text that Enoch sees himself in the role of the Chosen One and the Son of Man, but some scholars believe this idea was not part of the original text but was tacked on later.

One of the interesting things about this book is chapters 41-44, where the angel shows Enoch all the secrets—identical to those revealed to people by the Watchers and designated as forbidden knowledge: secrets of thunder and lightning, including how to tell by the sound of the thunder whether the lightning is for a blessing or a curse, winds and where they were kept, the storehouses of hail and mist, the secrets of clouds and dew, the mysteries of the sun and moon (bright to the righteous and dark to the sinner) and how steadfast these celestial objects are. The angel also reveals to Enoch the names of all these entities, and as we know, the knowledge of the secret name of an entity gives one power over it. But notice that because Enoch is righteous and a righteous angel is revealing these secrets to him, he is not in any way faulted for acquiring this knowledge (which is condemned as forbidden or corrupt when the Watchers share it with humans). Quite the contrary—Enoch is given these secrets because he is righteous, not because the angel wants to get something out of him, like the Watchers seemingly did with people (in fact, we do not know what the Watchers' motivation was in sharing these secrets with people).

The emphasis on the condemnation of the Watchers for revealing forbidden secrets to human beings is emphasized in Similitudes. The idea that their teachings are corrupting is important in this book, even though it is not much mentioned in the rest of Enoch. The Watchers' sexual transgression is not the big sin here, and we never hear about any bastard transspecies children who wreck the world either—although the "violence of the satans" is mentioned, who they are is not explained. In fact, instead of the Nephilim's rapaciousness, cannibalism, and bestiality causing the Earth itself and the souls of the human dead to cry out to Heaven, we are told that oppression of human beings comes about precisely because of people learning the angels' secrets.

The Evolution of the Watchers

This is especially true in the section called Noah's vision, chapter 65. Noah asks Enoch to tell him why the Earth has been shaking; Enoch informs him that God is going to let loose a flood that will destroy the world on account of how people have learned and used the secret knowledge shared by the Watchers: sorcery, brightly colored clothes, metal images (instead of clay ones), and how to smelt silver, lead, and tin. A special emphasis is placed on the evil of sorcery. Nothing whatsoever is said about the Watchers taking wives, the wives' supposed uncleanness, or even if the wives tempted the Watchers, which becomes an important accusation in the Christian readings of this work.

Another text from the time of Similitudes is called Jubilees, which I will discuss later. But right now, I want to mention that Jubilees, like Similitudes, focuses on the corruption of humanity coming from the angels' teachings rather than their actions with women. However, Jubilees limits the Watchers' teaching to divination. Jubilees is, like Enoch, part of the canon of the Ethiopian church and was preserved in the form of excerpts in Christian chronicles. After the Talmud was completed, both Jubilees and Similitudes occur in Rabbinic discussions.

Besides the mention of "satans," we also have the beginning of the idea of the Devil in Similitudes, which is a somewhat foreign concept to Judaism, which features demons aplenty but generally no head devil. In Genesis, the snake that speaks to Eve is not identified with the devil. We have something approaching a devil in Similitudes in terms of the Watcher Gadre'el (Enoch 69:6), who teaches humans how to use the metal weapons of war (shields, swords, and chain mail) to kill people. We're told that he also led Eve astray. We know that the snake will be equated to the Devil later on, but at this time the idea that the snake was an angel or a devil is new.

Another curious bit in Similitudes is the lowering of the status of scribes. Remember that we are told that Enoch invented writing and was a scribe, but in Similitudes, it is one of the Watchers who invented writing, pens, ink, and paper, and he is condemned for corrupting humanity through this. In a way, this fits with the changing attitude about sin coming down from Adam and Eve. Writing is for transmitting knowledge, even the forbidden kind, and it could be that just as the Watchers are condemned for teaching the forbidden knowledge of the stars, clouds, winds, and so on but it's okay for Enoch to learn these things, the writing that Penume (one of the Watchers) invents is specifically focused on transmitting forbidden knowledge. Later on, in Jubilees, another Enochian work, we do get a story about a man who is corrupted because he is able to learn the secrets of reading the stars from some writing that had been carved into a stone.

Also, remember that it was fruit of the Tree of the Knowledge of Good and Evil that Adam and Eve ate. This knowledge threatened Heaven—God wanted them hurriedly evicted from the Garden before they ate from the Tree of Eternal Life and became like the Elohim. That forbidden knowledge also enabled humans to move forward into their own free will and to reproduce themselves, but as dangerous as knowledge is, it also allowed death to come into being. Knowledge throughout Enoch is a double edged sword.

Similitudes and Abortion: A Pop Connection

I have seen memes online depicting pseudo-ancient figures with metal instruments like forceps aborting a fetus and blaming this on the demons that were the Nephilim (or their souls, I guess), basing this claim on Enoch 69:12, which is part of Similitudes. There we are told how a Watcher by the name of Kasdeya taught people various ways to "smite" others, including how to smite embryos. But what people propagating these memes don't know is that these "smitings" or "blows" are not physical; they are not the surgical instruments of abortion but precisely the metaphysical attacks of malevolent magic.

This "blow" is not aimed at the womb of a woman who does *not* want to bring the fetus to term; instead, it is aimed at the woman who *does* want to bring the fetus to term, one who looks forward to having a baby, not one hoping for a miscarriage or abortion. This concept of spiritual attack with physical results has a lot in common with the attacks by spirits in other cultures, such as the Anglo-Saxon concept of elfshot. That was an illness that usually involved pain or cramps resulting from invisible arrows shot by elves in the British Isles. The targets were usually people or livestock.

There is nothing unique about this "smiting" in The Book of Enoch, nothing prophetic, nothing that describes the surgical operation known as abortion. The very idea that Similitudes describes demons performing abortions is anti-historical; just for starters, there were no surgical abortions at that time. Also, one of the greatest preoccupations in Jewish talisman-making is the protection of the pregnant woman from demonic attack that might result in a miscarriage, and this kind of talisman making goes back to ancient times. Fear of and protection from this kind of supernatural attack on the fetus is as far from abortion as the sun is from the moon. I can't make it any clearer. All I can say is people who get their prophecy from memes are fools, learning from people who are completely ignorant about ancient texts.

CHAPTER EIGHT

The Astronomical Book

The Astronomical Book was written in the third century BCE at the latest. Scholars believe that The Book of the Watchers was put together at the same time or a little later. Besides the Hebrew Bible, these are the oldest Jewish writings that have been found.

The Ethiopic version of this book is much shorter than the Aramaic version that was eventually found in Qumran. Also, the Ethiopic version doesn't contain the calendar or the astronomical and meteorological info that the Aramaic version does. On the other hand, the Aramaic fragments from Qumran don't contain chapters 80–81 that are in the Ethiopic version, which tell how nature's order has been deformed due to human actions, among other things. Thanks to the discovery of the Aramaic version of this book at Qumran, we now know that ancient Jews had an extensive knowledge and lore about astronomy, the foundation of the universe, and angels as far back as the third century BCE.

What's odd is that the information in these two books, the oldest in Enoch, isn't mentioned in the Hebrew Bible; Genesis is about a thousand years older. However, just because it is not written down does not mean the knowledge didn't exist. The Astronomical Book and The Watchers share an interest in how the universe works, especially with respect to the stars (remember that the Watchers are literally guardians of the stars) and the sun and the moon. This makes these works unique in terms not only of other Enochic works but with respect to the Hebrew Bible. They were both written by groups of scribes who saw a religious connection between astronomy, the map of the heavens, and geography. Even though this book says that the fact that the stars follow certain paths and schedules is proof that they are divinely ordered, that the stars' paths and schedules have been carefully observed and kept track of shows the writers' scientific bent.

This sort of interest is not evidenced in the Hebrew Bible, and some scholars believe that this kind of observation implies that the scribes who wrote these books were not part of any anti-establishment group because the constant observation and notation of the stars requires social stability, time, and space to track such celestial movements. However, some scholars might make this argument precisely because earlier scholars of Enoch did connect it to anti-establishment groups—without providing any written evidence of this connection—which would make later scholars critique a story about the book's history that is based on nothing at all.

The type of astronomy described in The Astronomical Book is most likely connected to the kind that was used in Mesopotamia a couple of centuries before this book was written. What's interesting is that its writers didn't make use of Greek knowledge of the stars. We must ask why not. Perhaps they simply rejected any contemporary knowledge and preferred to reach back into the past for it. It could be that they simply rejected the Hellenization of their culture, or maybe they just didn't know about Hellenic views of the stars.

Some scholars say that this must be a question of rejecting Greek astronomy for nationalist reasons. But the Greeks didn't consider that astronomy had anything to do with the divine; it was simply observation and math. When we remember just how important knowledge is when it is connected to the divine in Enoch—and that forbidden knowledge that leads to sin and destruction is bad precisely because it is disassociated from the divine—we can see that it would be logical for the composers of Enoch to reject what they might well see as a soulless practice like simple observational astronomy.

Some have said that since Greek astronomy is rejected in this book, that the people who wrote The Astronomical Book and who compiled Enoch must have been separatist in terms of the Hellenized society of the land of Israel at the time of writing. I don't think that's so convincing, especially since the same argument about separatism was made for so long about Enoch and then was shown to be false. Instead, it seems more likely that the goal of using astronomy in Enoch is not so much about predicting where stars and planets might go in the sky but for determining where good and bad people, bad angels, God, and bad and good stars are located.

There's no evidence that the astronomical system in this book was Ptolemaic either, since that system wasn't created until 150 CE, centuries after The Astronomical Book was composed. It must have arisen in an ancient Near Eastern system instead.

Besides astronomy, The Astronomical Book concerns itself with the calendar, focusing on the solar version. This is the calendar used by the sacrificial cult in Jerusalem before the exile to Babylon occurred. The elite who returned from Babylon—a group dominated by priests— brought with them the lunar calendar that was used in Babylon and replaced the solar calendar that had previously determined the times of all the festivals with a lunar calendar, which resulted in all sorts of awkwardness in determining when a festival should be observed. (By the way, the lunar calendar that they brought back with them from Babylon is still influential on the Jewish calendar today—the same names of the months are used, and each month begins on a new crescent moon).

At the time of the writing of Enoch, the calendar's wonkiness was thought to be caused by human evil; in this worldview, human behavior affects the natural world (this always reminds me of how simple observation of subatomic particles deforms their path). We see this noted in chapter 80 of Enoch. The Astronomical Book argues against the Babylonian calendar of 360 days in favor of a solar calendar that is 364 days long with one extra or intercalary day. This latter calendar makes the festivals occur on the same day every year. However, The Astronomical Book doesn't overtly argue against the "new" calendar used in the Temple. In the past, some scholars have said that the 364-day year was from cuneiform sources, but others have completely rejected this. In fact, the 364-day calendar The Astronomical Book proposes is much older than the Babylonian one.

The lunar "gates" in The Astronomical Book are not related to the Mansions of the Moon in other systems, which apparently was developed in the Babylonian system. The lunar gates in The Astronomical Book don't coincide with any zodiacal signs but are about the relationship between the moon and the sun.

In terms of forbidden and allowable knowledge, secret or otherwise, we know that the Watchers brought the forbidden knowledge of astronomy down to Earth and shared it with human beings, to their detriment. How different is the knowledge of the stars embodied in the calendar in terms of how it is acquired by Enoch. He learned it by Uriel breathing on him, which to me immediately brings to mind the creation of Adam. However, I think it's worth pointing out that not only does The Astronomical Book not talk about the forbidden secrets that the Watchers taught— it doesn't even mention their names. To me this hints that this book and The Watchers arose in different milieux and didn't know of each other.

The Dream Visions

The Book of Dream Visions isn't concerned with occupations like astronomy; instead, it focuses on Jewish history, especially in the works it's composed of—The Apocalypse of Weeks and The Animal Apocalypse. The Maccabean Revolt was a particular focus, and the work has a militaristic and nationalist flavor that is new compared to the other books that make up Enoch. It was composed when Daniel, for which oracular dreams are also important, was being written and edited. This was during the time of the Maccabean Rebellion in 164 BCE.

Remember that this rebellion was especially focused on foreign influences and impositions on Judaism, particularly in terms of Hellenism, but you can see how the rejection of foreign imports into Judaism would harken back to Babylonian influences on the sacrificial cult of Jerusalem as well. Those priests and members of the Jerusalem elite who had been taken to Babylon subsequently returned to Jerusalem with Babylonian wives and a lot of Babylonian customs, including religious ones. For that reason, even as the Second Temple began to be built, there were many who thought the sacrificial cult could not be correctly reconstituted.

Animal Apocalypse

The Animal Apocalypse, which is part of The Dream Visions and is associated with the Asael story, can also be interpreted as a metaphor for the predatory, corrupting nature of foreign influences and of the priesthood. The scholar Boccaccini believes that Enoch reflects dissent in the priesthood itself due to issues of ritual purity and the use of a lunar calendar instead of the original solar one. This critique of the Temple priesthood might seem pretty radical for the time that produced Enoch, but if we read the Prophets, we see even in more ancient times, people were criticizing the actions of the Temple priesthood for importing Babylonian practices like astrology as well as putting up Asherahs inside the Temple itself as well as in in High Places (local places of worship). Asherah was an ancient partner of YHVH in the Land of Israel and Judea. Some have connected her with Eve or have viewed the Shekhinah as one of her forms. Ordinary people were building their own local temples in order to avoid having to travel to Jerusalem for rituals and paying the priests for sacrifices and we see in Enoch various references to the main competitor to the Temple of Jerusalem, the Golden Calf temples in the north of the Land of Israel.

The Animal Apocalypse was written probably a bit before the Maccabean Revolt, around 200 BCE. This puts it after The Watchers was completed, which is a major influence on it, and it was then finished during the rebellion. Aramaic fragments of this work were discovered at Qumran. The use of animals in divinatory dreams goes back to prophetic works centuries before.

The Astronomical Book

The Animal Apocalypse is written as if it were Enoch's dream, which he tells to his son Methuselah. This type of dream and the incorporation of symbolic animals makes it like some of the oracles in Daniel (Dan 7, 8, 10–12). Daniel interprets his dreams, but Enoch doesn't.

Logically enough, in this work, various animals represent individual characters and groups of people. The sheep, shown as blind, represent the Israelites; they gain their sight at the end of time, when a new temple arises as a new layer above the old (polluted) one. This temple is so big that all the people of Israel can fit inside it; this is not the exclusivist Temple that existed at the time the book was written.

If the sheep are ordinary Israelites, the white bulls and cows represent named characters like Adam and Eve, and the black bulls and cows stand for people who have sinned, like Cain and his descendants. Abel and Ham, who is Noah's second son, are neutral red bulls and cows; they are not important to the story. The women who had sex with the Watchers are symbolized by black cows. The Watchers themselves are represented as stars (which symbol keys this into other parts of Enoch). Their children are portrayed as wild animals, like camels and jackasses.

In this version of the Watchers story, the women are innocent victims. They don't seduce the angels, but neither do the angels teach them any secrets or forbidden knowledge. That means this is a pretty different take on the Watchers story, especially when compared to versions that come after, where the sexual sins of the angels are glossed over, people spread the angels' forbidden knowledge—which leads to rampant sin—and the women eventually are even accused of seducing the angels instead of, at best, being seduced by the angels and at worst, raped by them.

The Animal Apocalypse is related to the Book of Daniel. It uses the name the colonizers gave to the Land of Israel—Palestine—which is like calling the land of the Oswego nation Oklahoma. Even so, the author of this work does not care about the history of empires; they are only interested in the history of the righteous, of Israel, and of the Temple.

It's in The Animal Apocalypse that we are told that Asael was the first Watcher to come down to Earth, but to repeat, no mention of his teachings is made in this part of the book. Even so, the blame is on human beings for the decline of human behavior and the increasing destruction of the Earth.

Another difference in this version of the Watchers story is that the Giants (aka Nephilim) are all destroyed in the Flood. This cuts the cord between the pre-Flood Nephilim and modern-day demons which are the spirits of 10 percent of the Nephilim who were preserved precisely to nettle human beings.

PART TWO

CHARACTERS
IN ENOCH

CHAPTER NINE

Enoch: Man and Something More

Enoch, as the individual who we are told received wisdom and invented writing, came about at least a century before The Book of Enoch was written (that is, in the 4th to 3rd centuries BCE or earlier). Some scholars think the figure of Enoch was based on an older Mesopotamian mythical person, but that idea might be not so much a historical fact but the result of what was once very common among researchers of Jewish ancient texts—always looking for some earlier "original" foreign stories as sources, as if the Israelites could not have created their own mythology. I've noticed this occurs quite a bit in popular modern interpretations of ancient Hebrew texts. This is called "source seeking" and is no longer an acceptable prejudice among scholars of the ancient world.

Although Enoch is often connected with Ezekiel, who is a prophet in the canon of the Hebrew Bible and whose vision inspired other visions, and both are designated as "son of man" (*ben adam*), there are a number of differences between them. Usually, prophets are given their initial vision or mission at a particular place on Earth that is named. There are named places in Enoch's story, but he receives his gift of prophecy or mission in Heaven, not on Earth. He is the only prophet who has that experience, so there is something quite special about him, although we never really find out exactly what that is. When Enoch is called to prophesy in chapters 14–16, the scene has similarities to Ezekiel 1, but Enoch receives this call and is taken up to Heaven while Ezekiel gets his call on Earth.

When Ezekiel condemns the priestly doings at the Temple, he also describes how this ritual pollution can be remedied and how the sacrificial cult should be practiced correctly. Enoch condemns priestly intercourse with menstruating women but doesn't describe how this ritual impurity can be fixed. He just points it out and condemns it. It is as if underlying the text is the thread that the Temple of Jerusalem cannot be fixed. To me, this points in two directions—to the Temples of the Golden Calf in the North or to some temple in the future that is metaphorical or spiritual.

The hint of the importance of a different location for the Temple is given right before Enoch goes up to Heaven to read the Watchers' petition for mercy directly to God (13:7). He goes to sit by the waters of Dan in the land of Dan, south of Mount Hermon and to the west. There he recites the Watchers' petition for mercy until he falls asleep. This is exactly where Jeroboam's Temple of the Golden Calf was built. Hmm.

In Isaiah 6, we are told that the feet of God rest in the Temple of Jerusalem, yet Enoch travels up to a Heaven that is not over Jerusalem but over this alternative temple at the foot of Mount Hermon. Not only is this Heaven and the Divine not located over Jerusalem but not even over Mount Zion, which is referred to as the holy mountain in other parts of the book (26:2), but here it is not even mentioned.

Not only is Enoch different from other prophets (not least of all by having been lifted up to Heaven by God and becoming some kind of extraordinary individual who is more than human), he can even do things that angels like the Watchers can't do. Once the Watchers leave Heaven and have sex with human beings, the Watchers cannot return to Heaven just like Adam and Eve cannot return to the Garden. But Enoch can travel between Earth and Heaven repeatedly. He even goes back to Earth for three years before returning to Heaven, and we see in the story of Methuselah's questioning of him that he can later make quick trips down to the "far corners" of the Earth to respond to Methuselah's questions. Likewise, once he is in Heaven, he can go to the palace of fire and ice and look at God's face, something which neither angels nor humans can do (until later works).

Enoch is also extraordinary in the kind of splitting he experiences in Heaven. When he sees that place, he sees another figure who looks like a man but whose face is as full of grace as an angel (46:1). An angel who is piloting him around tells him that the figure he sees is the Chosen One, the Son of Man, and he has various tasks (46:2–8). His job will be to smash kings and the powerful for oppressing the righteous, whom he will champion. At the end of Similitudes, Enoch discovers that this character is himself. To me, this has implications for our own responsibility for healing the universe.

CHAPTER TEN

The Watchers:
Angels and
Something Less

The Watchers are an order of angels. Although some of them came down to Earth to take human wives, others remained up in Heaven and continued to stay at their posts and be holy; both groups are referred to as Watchers whether they are good or bad. This name first appears in an Aramaic section of Daniel, in chapter 4; there, they are holy angels. Their name seems a reference to the fact that they never sleep, but I wondered if also they might have that name because they watched women on Earth below. They act as guards, but they are also related to or responsible for astronomical events.

Often they are connected with the stars, especially since in Enoch, there are steadfast stars that people are advised to imitate because they always follow the paths that God has set out for them. In contrast, there are bad stars who don't follow their divinely directed paths and by doing so, create havoc with human attempts to abide by the commandments about observing festivals. Those stars, Enoch learns, have a special dark prison as a "reward." The Watchers who take human wives end up in similar prisons.

I think one of the reasons why the Watchers were so condemned was perhaps not so much because they took human wives, although this is certainly mentioned and fits with the many commandments involving the prohibition against mixing things (in this case, species, for there is no commandment against angels and people having sex or marrying), but because they left their posts. The stars are left without guidance due to the departure of the Watchers, and they progressed in unpredictable ways that interfered with piety, since times of year for festivals was thrown off, and caused calendars to come into use that were wonky and just plain wrong.

Although illustrations now show the fallen angels as demonic, with bat wings or even horns, the fallen Watchers were never referred to or considered demons in Enoch. They were sinners, not demons, and that is how ancient Jews considered them. The idea that they were demons or became demons on account of their sins was created by Christians centuries after Enoch was written. Even so, they are not called demons even in the Gospels. One of the issues could have been that the Greek translations might refer to them as daimons, which is not a demon in Greek mythology but just a spirit of, for instance, a great person who guides the living, spirits who represent abstract things, or forces of nature. They were not gods, and in that sense, they have a certain commonality with angels. They were seen as protective rather than evil and as helping people rather than leading them into wrongdoing or bedeviling them.

There is a curious bit in Enoch 19:1–2 which is somewhat ambiguous in terms of the angels and their relationship to the demonic. We are told that "their spirits" have brought destruction to human beings and lead them to worshiping demons as if they were gods, and that this will continue until the end of time. But it's clear from the rest of the book that the ones who brought destruction to human beings were the Nephilim, and it is the spirits of 10 percent of the Nephilim who (for the most part, depending on which part of the book you are reading) will survive the Flood precisely in order to lead human beings into idolatry, so I don't believe it is in keeping with the book to categorize the fallen Watchers as demons.

In subsequent writings, such as The Testament of Solomon,[49] we come across a most well-known demon, Asmodeus, who says that he was the son of a woman and one of the Watchers. This is the demon whom King Solomon tricked into helping him build the Temple. In turn, Asmodeus managed to exchange places with Solomon and ruled in his stead for some years, until Solomon overcame him and imprisoned him in a rock (echoes of what happens to the fallen Watchers). In later works, Asmodeus is considered a demon of lust, which to me again hearkens back to the reason why demons exist in the post-Flood Enochian world.

The Watchers are condemned because of their lust for women, but we are also told in chapter 16 that they taught humans forbidden subjects and even that the information they gave humans was corrupted and corrupting. However, the real cause of their offense flickers between lust, mixing of separate categories (human and angel), sharing secret info, info that was corrupted, and info that corrupted human beings. There is a constant shifting between those four "sins" throughout Enoch, with now one and now the other moving to the foreground or being invisible. One thing is clear—it was because the Watchers knew so much that they were able to create havoc on earth by sharing that knowledge.

The first mention of a rebellion of angels in Heaven who are then defeated, literally fall to earth, and become demons or devils is by Tatian the Assyrian (120–180 CE). A convert from Paganism to Christianity, he was a student of Justin Martyr and later formed his own Christian school, but he ended up being expelled from the Church for advocating celibacy and vegetarianism. He taught that it was precisely demons who convinced people to be polytheistic. He equates the Greek gods with demons and lists all the skills the Greeks have, which just so happen to coincide with the forbidden knowledge the fallen Watchers taught: dream divination, reading the flights of birds, astrological fortune-telling, metallurgy, writing, and more. Tatian describes in his work *Oratio ad Graecos* how God banished the leader of the rebellious angels, who was followed by an army of other rebellious angels to live on earth as demonic influences on humans.

Eventually, the "sons of Elohim"—the Watchers—were no longer considered to have been angels by Jewish or Christian authorities.

The Leaders of The Watchers: Asael and Shemihazah

Two separate stories (which have never been found in stand-alone versions, even though some scholars believe they existed separately in ancient times) are combined in the heart of The Watchers, which is chapters 6-11 of Enoch. If we look at Asael and Shemihazah, the two major leaders of the Watchers, we can learn a lot about what was considered forbidden knowledge and how it affected human beings.

These two strands tell different stories rather than duplicating one story. Some consider that the Shemihazah story is about sexual transgression and the story of Asael is about how revealing forbidden knowledge is at the root of the corruption of the Earth. The two stories have a uniting element—blood. The Shemihazah story focuses on how, through their action of sex with women, children are born who commit great bloody violence. Asael teaches how to make the weapons of war, which of course implies bloodshed, but his knowledge goes also into the making of female ornamentation, which leads to the blood "spilled" in ritually impure sex acts: women entice others to have sex with them while they are menstruating.

One interesting take on these two different stories being bundled together here is that their differences are intentional. This fits in with what I've mentioned about ancient texts allowing for competing and contradictory voices in a way that modern texts do not.

Asael

Let's start with Asael, even though his strand in the story is thought to be later than that of Shemihazah. But it makes sense to me to start with him because his knowledge on the face of it was much more deadly: he was the one who taught humans the secrets of metal-working, which they used to make swords, shields, and chain mail rather than plows, shovels, hoes, and trowels. What's odd about Asael is that he was not the one who introduced metal-working to humans in terms of the much older book, Genesis. That was Tubal-Cain (Genesis 4:22–24), and that man did not acquire that knowledge from angels. Tubal-Cain was in the generation directly after Enoch but from the line of Cain rather than that of Seth, who was Enoch's ancestor. We never hear where Tubal-Cain got his knowledge. To me the implication is that he developed it out of his own practice. In contrast, Asael didn't develop metal-working out of his practice but acquired the secret knowledge in Heaven and then revealed it to human beings.

A few scholars believe that Asael is a morph of Prometheus, one of the Titans, the ancestors of the Olympic pantheon, who brought fire to humans. He tricked Zeus into choosing a sacrifice that was not as nourishing—bones wrapped in fat instead of meat wrapped in an ox's stomach—and in retaliation, Zeus took fire from humans. Prometheus brought it back. Zeus then had him chained to a rock where an eagle would arrive every day and eat his liver. In later stories, Prometheus was freed by Herakles.

I guess you could say that as a Titan and not an Olympian, Prometheus was more like an angel than like God Almighty. He didn't bring metalworking down to Earth, but he brought the means to do metalworking—fire. In a later version of the story, he also brings writing, math, farming, science, and medicine; however, none of these are the all-important metalworking or magic. He ends up chained to a rock as happens to the Watchers but unlike them, who at best will be freed in the end of time to burn forever, he later is freed by Heracles, who was half-god and half-human. No eternal fire involved.

For me, there are simply too many differences between these two figures to see Asael as a copy of Prometheus. There is nothing whatsoever about Prometheus having sex with human women or fathering hybrids that prey on humans, shed massive amounts of blood, engage in cannibalism and bestiality, and just make such a mess of things that the Flood is necessary to get rid of them. Nor does Prometheus' gift of fire corrupt humans and cause war-making and sexual offenses. Instead, it helps them.

I've mentioned "source seeking." Sometimes scholars of ancient Hebrew texts really stretch to obliterate any originality in these stories. They are always looking for some "original" version that never resides in Israelite culture. In more recent times, this has come to be seen as a problem in the study of ancient Israelite culture.

Going back to Asael, instead of focusing on the fact that instruments of war would naturally cause a lot more havoc and death on Earth than, for instance, makeup, we see highlighted not the deadly knowledge of making war materials but instead how women learned from him how to decorate themselves with jewelry, gems, flashy clothing, and makeup, thus enticing the angels and other humans to have sex with them. The combination of metalworking and making gems and colors fits with ancient alchemy, but on the other hand, even though eye shadow in this time and place was antimony, a metal, and the alchemists were known for making artificial gems and coloring gold, which would fit with making jewelry, I haven't heard of them making dyes for clothing. The fact that the presents for women come in for special castigation compared to weapons of death makes me think that that whole aspect was tacked on later.

In the Shemihazah version, the women are innocent, but not in the Asael version. Instead, they are as guilty as the Watchers themselves in terms of corrupting human beings. This seems to have something in common with the placing of magic as a foreign incursion that is brought into Israel by women who also practice witchcraft. The idea that women seduced the Watchers by heightening their natural beauty with artifice occurs in other Enochic works and in later Rabbinic writings that make use of earlier stories.

One of the things that has surprised me—and I guess it really shouldn't have, in retrospect—was how the attitudes towards what the Watchers taught humans changed over the years and how gradually the sin of lust or of mixing categories that should remain separate (angels and humans) was gradually eclipsed by a focus on what the Watchers taught and to whom and how that affected the world. Yes, the idea that it was angels who brought evil to the Earth was, to me, radical, but I thought once having fielded that idea, it would either continue to be influential or would be simply wiped out. Even though nowadays it's common for people to claim that Enoch was suppressed, I think I've provided good evidence that it wasn't. It just fell out of use because it no longer reflected what the majority believed. Maybe it was difficult for people to wrap their head around the concept that evil did not originate with humans once everyone got on the Adam and Eve train. For me, though, there is something just a little bit arrogant about thinking that humans invented evil on Earth. Yes, I do believe that 99 percent of the evil done is by humans, with no help whatsoever from demons or devils, but I also think that perhaps there is much more to how the power of evil sorts itself out than that it's just some people being bad. And of course, who allows a tenth of the souls of the evil Nephilim to persist in the world? Not humans. God.

Shemihazah

Shemihazah's story was written before at least 200 BCE. It's been found in three Aramaic manuscripts in Qumran. In contrast to Asael, who taught people how to make material objects, Shemihazah taught metaphysical workings like magic and astrology as well as root-cutting, which although it involves actual material (plants), is dependent on actions related to the stars to work, and so the forbidden knowledge of how stars influence which plants and when is important. Some scholars believe that the Shemihazah story was a kind of parody of the Diadochi,[50] who claimed divine ancestry, or that it depicts pre-Flood warrior kings. This would, I suppose, fit with some interpretations of the Nephilim that see them as warriors, but to me neither of these ideas is convincing and what's more, they don't seem pertinent.

An early Christian writer, Athenagoras,[51] discusses the story of the Watchers in his Legatio 25, 1–3. There he says that even in his day, the spirits of the angels inspired lust and the demons (the spirits of the Nephilim) inspired violence. He names Shemihazah as the Prince of Matter, which puzzles me since that figure is all about the metaphysical—it's Asael who teaches people how to transmute and make things—but it is certainly true from the Greek perspective that matter is where evil lives. So perhaps from Athenagoras' perspective, where you have evil, you have matter. It's also true that to have sex with women, the angels had to transform themselves into men, that is, matter. If you already had an evil inclination in spirit form, morphing into a material form might well empower it, if you believe that matter is the home for evil.

Just as with Asael, some scholars have said that the Shemihazah story might be influenced by Greek myths, especially *Titanomachia*, a now lost epic poem of ancient Greece that told of a great battle between the Titans and the Olympians, led by Zeus. The thing that is most striking about this is that neither the Titans nor the Giants are the children of gods and women, and they are not the oppressors of humankind who merited the world being destroyed by the Flood. So to me, this parallel doesn't work either. It's perfectly fine to stretch a story a bit, but you cannot turn a sock into an overcoat.

Just as with Asael, some compare Shemihazah with Prometheus, but in my opinion, the same problems are even more prevalent here, since Shemihazah taught people magic and astrology, nothing like teaching about fire or even the alchemical arts.

What the Individual Watchers Taught

I've put together a chart based on various sources with respect to Enoch which lists the twenty Watchers who were the leaders of the other Watchers who came to Earth. Each had a specialty that is loosely indicated by their name. Some of these bodies of secret knowledge are identical to the practices that the prophet Isaiah ascribes to Babylon, which he represents in his writings as a seductive woman. These bodies of forbidden knowledge include spellcasting, sorcery, reading the stars, weather magic, and moon divination.

In various books of the Bible, including Leviticus, Deuteronomy, Nahum, Isaiah, and Ezekiel, magical arts are attacked and identified as foreign practices that intruded into Israel from Canaan, Babylonia, and Assyria. Babylon and Nineveh, the biggest Assyrian city at one time, are said to be the sources of this foreign magic. The Babylonian astrologers, diviners, and wise men in fact practiced the same skills. This same group of skills is given in the earliest Jewish magic book we know of, *Sefer ha-Razim* (*The Book of Secrets*), but that book focuses on angels who inhabit the seven levels of Heaven (referred to as the Palaces in a large body of work). *Sefer ha-Razim* is a pre-Kabbalistic magical text that was written in Hebrew between the late 3rd and early 4th centuries CE. It describes angels associated with the seven heavens who might be adjured to heal illness, give the gift of prophecy, acquire wealth, or even to destroy one's enemies. They are also listed in Jubilees 2:2.

I have not included other lists of angels that occur in Enoch; the list I give here appears in the oldest part of the book. Other lists can be seen as incorporated from other works, times, and places, and at least one list gives names that are not found anywhere in Jewish magic either of the time or any time later and might have been Babylonian. Further, none of the angels mentioned in that list is part of any of the events of the book. Those angels are condemned not for what they teach but for revealing secret knowledge. That list gives the sense of being thrown in for effect—to make the work seem more a product of hidden knowledge, an effect I have certainly noticed in various esoteric works from all sorts of cultures and times. One scholar refers to this as "mystery terminology," words that are in a text specifically in order to give the audience the impression that the author has experienced esoteric processes that have revealed to the writer images, words, and stories that hint at the deeply hidden, ultimate truths of the universe.

Each of the angels mentioned in the table below is a teacher of a body of forbidden knowledge that is related to their name, and most of the skills are connected to magic or divination—except for Asael, whose skill is very practical. To me, this fits with the idea that Asael's story was separate from Shemihazah's. Some of these angel names are mentioned in later sources of Jewish adjuration magic, and that implies they were not thought to be demons. I would consider that those can be adjured today, but the rest are unknown.

The Watchers: Angels and Something Less

Name	Meaning	Subject Taught
Shemihazah	The name sees, or my name has seen	Magic involving the use of names, like curses, oaths, and spells, but also using Divine Names for magic. Root-cutting
Arteqoph	The earth is mighty	Signs related to the earth, especially land and weather magic
Remashel/Ramt'el	Burning ashes of God	Reading the signs of volcanoes and the land
Kokabel	Star of God	Astronomy and astrology
Oramel/Armumahel	God is their light	Reading celestial signs to do with light
Ramel	Thunder of God	Storm magic
Daniel	God is my judge	Learning God's judgment by divination
Ziqel	Lightning-flash of God	Reading the signs of lightning, shooting stars, and fire-balls
Baraqel	Lightning of God	Weather magic, especially lightning
Asael	God has made/done	Creation secrets
Hermani	Being of Hermon (mountain of curses)	Curse magic, pacts
Matarel	Rain of God	Rain magic
Ananel	Cloud of God	Reading clouds and weather signs
Setawel/Sithwa'el	Winter of God	Secrets of the calendar and seasons
Samshiel/Simsel	Sun of God	Secrets of the calendar and stars, especial to do with the sun
Sahriel (not the same as Sariel)	Moon of God (*sahar* is Aramaic word for Moon)	Secrets of the calendar and stars, especially to do with the moon

Name	Meaning	Subject Taught
Tummiel/Tammel	God has completed	Magic for bringing to completion or fruition
Turiel[52]	Mountain of God	Earth magic
Yamiel/Yomel	Sea of God	Sea magic
Yehadiel/Zehor'el	Brightness of God	Astronomical secrets

Spirits of The Watchers, Spirits of the Nephilim, and Demons

There's a bit of a kerfuffle as to whether it's the spirits of the Watchers or the spirits of the Nephilim which will continue to harass human beings and lead them into sin until the day of Judgment. However, I think the sentence in 19:1 is ambiguous enough to allow for the angel Uriel to be referring to the Watchers residing in the imprisonment the divine has set out for them (they are looking over at this scene) and when he says that these will go on to take various forms, harm people, convince them to worship demons as gods, that he is referring to the spirits of the Nephilim.

And Uriel said to me, "There stand the angels who mingled with the women. And their spirits—having assumed many forms, bring destruction on men and lead them astray to sacrifice to demons as to goods until the day of the great judgment, in which they will be judged with finality." (Enoch 19:1)

In Enoch 1–6 and in Jubilees, the "bastard spirits" that will continue to exist on earth and harass humans are the souls of the Nephilim, who were hybrids between angels and humans, and not the spirits or souls of the Watchers. In Jubilees 10:7–14, we learn that a tenth of the spirits of the Nephilim are allowed to remain as demons on Earth until the day of Judgment. The Watchers are incarcerated in an underground prison, where they will remain until the Judgment Day, although some believe that the demonic spirits of the Watchers roam over the Earth enticing humans to do evil even while their own bodies are locked in the ground.

However, we do come across some of these named Watchers in *Sefer ha-Razim* as angels that can be conjured. That fact undercuts them as demonic, since *Sefer ha-Razim* is about adjuring angels who are presently found on various levels of Heaven.

With respect to demons, we also have some non-Enochic Rabbinic stories of demons that were the offspring of Adam and Lilith before she left the Garden. We're also told that demons on Earth can break free from their eternal underground prisons when there is great tension in the supernatural world. In these stories, for instance, in Genesis Rabbah 24:6, we're told that both Adam and Eve created demon children but also that demons are the result of spirits who were made without a body before the first week of creation. The latter demons arose from the chaos (*tohu v'bohu*) that existed before Creation; the relationship between evil and chaos is strong. At the end of time, they will be thrown back into the abyss. These demons also went on to have sex with Adam and Eve separately and they produced more demons this way.

In terms of Enoch, however, demons are spirits of the Nephilim, end of story. There are no orders of demons like there are of angels, and in Enoch, they have no leader. They are differentiated only by what they do—their actions—but they are all the same type of creature.

In Enoch 16:1 and Jubilees 10:1–11, we learn that God allows (and if we speak plainly, has created) evil on Earth in the form of these demons which God permits to harass humans until the end of time; they can be exorcised but not destroyed until that day. They are legitimate in that they have a divine task—to test humans.

From the day of the slaughter and destruction and death of the giants, from the soul of whose flesh the spirits are proceeding, they are making desolate without (incurring) judgment. Thus they will make desolate until the day of the consummation of the great judgement, when the great age will be consummated. It will be consummated all at once. —Enoch 16:1

In the book of Jubilees, Mastema is a spirit of some unclear type—not a fallen Watcher and not a spirit of a dead Naphal (singular of Nephilim). He is not an incarnation of evil but has the job of marshaling the spirits of the Nephilim. He asks God to preserve 10 percent of them (Jubilees 10) so that they might harass people until the day of judgment, and God grants his request. His work is then divinely sanctioned. It is usual in Qumran sacred texts for adversaries like Mastema to do God's work. Since these evil spirits have God's permission to do what they do, dualism (good vs. evil, in this case) doesn't exist in the system. Also, some believe that if a demon doesn't have an opposite number among the angels, then the system is not dualistic.

At any rate, there is no story of the fall of Satan, which was adopted after the fourth century CE by Christians, that existed before the first century CE. So we know that this story is a purely Christian one and was not part of ancient Judaism or the Enochic works.

One reason why the Qumran sect might not have been too into the names of demons is that for one, they assumed that if you applied to join their sect, you were already demon-free. Second, they did not believe that the name of the demon was necessary to perform an exorcism. A hymn used to exorcise demons from a fragment from Qumran addresses "all the spirits of the angels of destruction and the spirits of the bastards, demons . . . Lilith, howlers." This is quite different from what we know of warding and exorcisms elsewhere in Judaism. Demons were often named, especially Lilith. But basically, all demons could be exorcised in the same way.

Also, nowhere in Enoch are demons and angels the same thing. The Watchers do wrong, and their actions prevent them from returning to Heaven, but they remain distinct from their hybrid children or the run-of-the-mill demons that evolved during Creation. This coincides with the perspective of the Qumran sect.

The Watchers: Angels and Something Less

However, the Christian Book of Revelation moves the story of the Watchers away from the time just before the Flood all the way back to the beginning of Creation and ties them to Satan and his colleagues (Revelation 12:9, Revelation 9:1, Luke 109:38). This view, of course, is not only not a part of Judaism but not a part of Enochic literature. This is not to say that it is wrong, but it is a major change from the original tales. The Satan story and his battle with Heaven coexists with the story of the Watchers until finally the Adam and Eve story as the origin of evil on Earth replaces the story of the role of the Watchers in bringing evil to Earth. It should be kept in mind that whenever one hears discussion about fallen angels, this doesn't indicate that any reference to the Watchers is meant.

CHAPTER ELEVEN

The Wives

Even though their role in the story of the Watchers gets small attention, the Watchers' wives become the targets of various misogynist perspectives through the history of The Book of Enoch. They are damned if they do and damned if they don't. If women are empowered by the Watchers' teachings—because magic is essentially an attempt at empowerment—then they are to blame for the terrible things that happened because they had the power to encourage those things to happen. But if they are seen as simple objects, it is just as bad, since then they are mere tools and in no way capable of resisting evil. I find them to be one of the most interesting groups in the book.

But we have to be careful when we look at ancient texts and peer under every word for misogyny or gender stereotypes; we might be revealing more about our own culture by doing that than demonstrating anything about the ancient culture we are studying. This becomes clearer as we look at all the ways the wives are viewed and must conclude that a simple binary perspective of masculine/feminine (or magic/religion) doesn't reveal as much as is there.

Women Are (Mostly) Not to Blame for
Evil Coming to Earth

The idea that women tempted the Watchers to come down to Earth and seduced them there does not fit with Enoch. If we go back to Similitudes, the archangels are responsible for not only leading Eve astray (as the snake) but teach humans weaponry, how to argue in order to deceive, how to write oaths, and bring illnesses that originate with demons: miscarriage, snakebite, and heatstroke. Women are the victims of the angels rather than their seducers in this view. We also see this in The Animal Apocalypse, where the cows (who symbolize women) are victims of the fallen stars— who represent the Watchers—and the Watchers' children (camels, asses, and other wild animals). However, the angels don't teach them anything. We don't even have any evidence that early users of Enoch thought of women as being particularly susceptible to and/or spreaders of magic the way they are portrayed in later times by some of those who edited, translated, and commented on Enoch.

Some scholars have seen the women in Watchers' story as objects because of the whole idea of the angels in Heaven literally watching them and seeing them as sex objects that they can go down to Earth to have sex with. Further on in the story, all the women do is give birth to the Nephilim. But what's left out of this perspective is that the Watchers share forbidden knowledge with their wives, and at least some of that is magic, which gives power over others and aspects of the world. This undercuts the idea that the wives are just things that the Watchers use.

We know that ancient Greeks often were fearful of women doing magic, especially if it was a case of women bewitching their husband to make him nicer. We might think that in the second century CE, during which Hellenization and Roman ideas about magic were common among Christians in those areas, that these Christians would see the women as being especially at fault for what happened to the Earth on account of their practicing magic—and indeed this does become the case later. But at that time, it was more common for Christians in Hellenized or Roman areas to see the real threat of magic coming from Pagans, especially if they worshiped multiple gods, used idols, and had animal sacrifice as part of their worship. When Christians create the story of the fallen angels and accuse them of bringing magic to humans, they see that as more of a practice of male heretics than of women.

Women's Culpability in Asael vs. Shemihazah Story

I've already touched upon the two different stories embedded in the Watchers legend. With respect to Asael, women learned how to pretty themselves up with jewelry, gems, bright clothing, and makeup and used these means to tempt people to sin with them. In the Shemihazah story, women are innocent, but in the Asael story, they bear some of the blame for the spreading of sin. This fits with the idea from the prophets that foreign women used magic and were seducers and corrupters of the Israelites.

Women might have been duped by the angels, basically tricked or conned into having sex with them without ever knowing what it would lead to, but they are culpable in that they help spread the Watchers' teaching of forbidden knowledge, which creates more evil on Earth. However, we have to notice that when Enoch condemns the Watchers for spreading unspeakable secrets, he says they told these secrets to women and it is through those secrets—using cosmetics, magic, incantation, binding and unbinding spells, root-cutting, divining through stars, lightning, the landscape, the sun, and the moon—that women *and* men multiplied evils on Earth. He doesn't confine the spreading of evil to women.

At one point we are told that these are "rejected mysteries." These are the direct opposite of the pretty much exact same secrets that Enoch has learned, but he learned them from God and from holy angels. The implication is that the means of learning is what makes those mysteries approved of or rejected. We don't see that the mysteries were rejected because they were taught to women.

Women Are the Problem at the Temple

In Judaism, blood is life; on the other hand, it's something that makes you ritually impure for a certain number of days. You must make yourself ritually pure again by bathing in "living" water, like from a spring or a river, and then you're pretty much good to go. To be clear, ritual impurity is

The Wives

not the same as moral impurity. Ritual impurity is due to things that just happen, like menstruation or ejaculation during dreams. Moral impurity is due to things you do of your own free will, such as having sex outside your marriage.

What does this have to do with foreigners? Surprisingly, a lot. If we go back to how some of the Prophets characterized foreign influence as corrupting and symbolized it as a foreign woman who practiced seduction and magic, we can interpret the wives in the Watchers story as representing a critique of the priests at the Temple of Jerusalem. Some of the most prominent scholars of The Book of Enoch have concluded that the Watchers' story serves the purpose of a critique of the priesthood of the Temple of Jerusalem—and I would add it could serve that critique even if the writers had never intended the story to have that meaning. If the priests of the Temple were having sex with women during their periods, then their children are illegitimate according to the law of ritual purity and then the line of the priesthood becomes delegitimized and the whole system topples. I think you can see how the Watchers story would fit with that particular critique.

Whether or not anyone was actually going around checking whether a priest's wife was having her period or not on which particular day, it could be a simple conflict of interpreting the laws of purity with respect to periods and to blood in general. It could have been as simple as one side saying, "wait X days after a woman's period is over to have sex" and the other side saying, "no, wait Y days." We don't know. This doesn't get settled until the Talmud, in tractate *Niddah* 1:1, which is long after the Temple had been destroyed and so it was no longer pertinent with respect to the priesthood.

Another bit of Enoch that some scholars believe indicates the book is meant as a critique of the priesthood of Jerusalem is Enoch's preference against Mount Zion, no matter that it is referred to as the holy mountain in 26:2. Instead of going there, he travels to a place that has not been polluted by the insertion of the worship of Zeus into the Temple or any corrupted priests—he goes to Dan and Mount Hermon in order to contact the angels and the divine.

We do find a couple of other documents that make this critique outright. One is the so-called Damascus Document, which was written around 100 BCE or a little earlier, so right around the time Similitudes was composed. Medieval copies were found in the Cairo Genizah[34] in fairly complete versions and original copies were also found in fragmented form at Qumran. It was a rule book directed at the Essenes, who lived in a camp outside of the Qumran community. This document specifically criticizes the Temple priesthood for not keeping apart from their wives during their period.

Another work from the same period—first to second century BCE—called The Psalms of Solomon says that the priests of the Temple were unclean through various means (which would, by the way, include masturbation) and that in addition through the ritual impurity of menstrual blood they contaminated the sacrifices that they offered, invalidating the whole process.

The other purity question might have nothing at all to do with menstrual blood and everything to do with the blood of lineage. The priests of the Temple of Jerusalem might well have married outside of priestly families for more than one generation while in Babylon. This also would delegitimize the priesthood, since it was by definition a hereditary one.

A note about blood in Judaism. It's not that blood is gross or disgusting and that's why men are not supposed to have sex with their wife during menstruation. After all, we are told that blood is life, and that's why we should not eat animal blood. Blood was splashed on the altar during the sacrificial cult; that wouldn't be done if blood was disgusting. Also, blood splashed on the doorposts protected the Israelites from the Angel of Death while they were in Egypt, so it's clearly powerful magic. In this worldview, it's more like menstrual blood represents a life that has been wasted, exactly the same way that ejaculate that lands outside of a woman's vagina is wasted. Both mean a life that could have been made has not been made.

The Wives

111

Remember the first commandment in the Hebrew Bible is "Be fruitful and multiply." To waste blood or ejaculate is a violation of that commandment. Having sex during menstruation also means the woman is quite a bit less likely to get pregnant, and we already know how important it is to be fruitful and multiply. Also, even if centuries later, religious authorities spoke of menstrual blood as if it were gross, that is a view they are imposing on the text. It didn't reside in the text itself.

The General Christian View of the Wives

What happened to the wives once they gave birth to the Nephilim? They aren't mentioned again except in the Greek versions of Enoch, where they become "sirens." We know from Greek mythology that the Sirens were responsible for bringing death to those who heard their song. Does the choice of this word indicate that the writer believed that the wives essentially brought death to those who interacted with them? That they destroyed the Watchers and/or brought death to the world by the havoc of their children and the resulting punishment of the Flood?

That the wives are morphed into creatures that lead men to their deaths is the way the wives are often seen in early Christian translations and exegeses of The Watchers. Just as Christians later interpreted Eve as caving to evil and then turning around to tempt weak-kneed Adam to succumb to evil (and so become evil herself), so the angels' wives are described as not just corrupted but corrupting—or even in some texts as tempting the Watchers while they were still in Heaven. Another version of the Watchers has them coming down to Earth not to get themselves human wives but to innocently teach human beings how to be good, and the women corrupt them, taking the Watchers' harmless gifts and perverting them—the skills of metalworking for making agricultural implements being turned to making jewelry, a prop for vanity, although notice that the much bigger perversion of metal-working is to forge the weapons of war. No one has ever died from the effects of makeup or jewelry, and yet it is precisely the skills dedicated to frippery that we are supposed to focus on and condemn instead of the skills of the armorer.

Byzantine Christian View of the Wives:
The Problem Is They Are Women

To get an idea of how attitudes towards women had changed after a few centuries rolled by, we can look at George Syncellus, who lived during the 8th century CE in Constantinople (now Istanbul in Turkey). We like to imagine that history is one great line moving upward, that history is about progress, but progress is far from inevitable. Syncellus is a good example. He came up with the idea that women enticed the Watchers down to Earth and ruined them with sex. He was very concerned with the deadly combination of women and magic and added the idea that the women made "hate charms" with the magical skills they gained from the Watchers. There is no basis for this in the original. For him, the real dangers to humans came from Asael's gifts—learning how to make shields, swords, and chain mail, jewelry, and cosmetics. According to him, these all lead to impiety. Perhaps, but the first three lead to death, unlike jewelry and cosmetics. It is as if being a seducer is as bad to Syncellus as being a killer.

This perspective is also reflected in the growing position that the angels were called Watchers not because they guarded the paths of the stars (this seems to be the original derivation of their name) but because they were up there watching women on Earth and being corrupted by what they saw. This fits with the Greek concept that objects seen send out particles to the eyes of those that view them, which helps bolster the idea that the women were enticing the Watchers.

The Two Christian Views of the Wives From Two Groups
of Christians

The Christians of Ethiopia had a completely different take on the outcome of the wives. In the Ethiopic manuscript, the wives become "peaceful," a curious choice of words. On the one hand, it makes one think that they will become silent—or dead. Or we can see this silence as a relief that their Watcher husbands have been removed from them, especially if we conceive of the Watchers as not "marrying" women but as "taking" them, that is, raping them. There certainly is a tradition in many cultures that women who have been raped are pilloried for having been victimized, blamed for it, and we are told in those cases that the raped woman "asked for it" in their flashy clothing, their makeup, their jewelry, or being in the wrong place at the wrong time. A familiar story. And this does seem to fit with some Christian perspectives of the wives as seducers.

Another Interpretation of the Wives' "Peace"

Another possibility is that instead of the wives haunting ruins and calling to men in order to kill them, maybe the trials of the wives are recognized as such. How, indeed, would it be to make love with an angel, even if it was consensual, and then find yourself giving birth to cannibalistic murdering giants who are responsible for bringing on the destruction of almost the entire world? And then to go on existing with those creatures as your "family" without any extraordinary powers but just as an ordinary human being? Sounds pretty horrible. Peace would mean being rescued from that situation. Further, the word "peaceful" as the definition of how the wives end up implies that they are not blamed in the Ethiopic translation for what occurred to them or to the world because of the actions of the angels or their children. Instead, they are given relief from the horrific events that they experienced.

We see here in the contrast between the wives' fate as becoming sirens on the one hand and peaceful on the other the demonstration of an enormous difference between two Christianities. In one, a Christianity of the Church, women are condemned for causing the behavior of others and therefore deemed responsible for the resulting destruction of the world. In contrast, the Ethiopic Orthodox Church was an outlying, distant peninsula of what would become Eastern Orthodoxy. We should keep the enormous difference between those two approaches to Christianity in mind when we are tempted to tar all Christians with the same brush, or worse, start wholesale condemning "Abrahamic" religions for brutality and stupidity.

The other thing is of course that the misogynist ideas about women's connections with magic don't originate in Christianity or Judaism but in ancient Greek (Pagan) culture. And in the Greek Christian translations of Enoch the link between women and magic is foregrounded. This fits nicely with Athenian condemnation of women practicing magic, especially if they were doing it to domesticate a husband. This misogyny also appeared in Jewish writers much under the sway of Hellenism, like Philo and Ben Sirah. Just because Hellenism looks back through its own lens of hatred for wives who dare to try to control a husband through magic does not mean we have to insert that behavior—and the disdain of it—into Enoch. However, in spite of this, we do not ever see the text changed so much that the wives end up locked in darkness or outright killed, like the Watchers or the Nephilim. The worst they encounter is to become sirens, which although they are deadly, are powerful.

The Wives

115

CHAPTER TWELVE

The Nephilim

One interesting parallel between the Watchers and the Nephilim is that neither of them can control their appetites. That lack of control is exactly how damage ends up being done to the inhabitants of the Earth, from humans to animals to fish and birds, and to the land itself. The teachings of the Watchers and the actions of their children bring about chaos on Earth.

Although the spirits of the Nephilim become demons, they don't typically torment people. Instead, they get them to worship idols. Oddly, the Nephilim are much more dangerous as living beings than as demons. It would be quite a stretch to compare their attempts to convince people to worship idols and perhaps lose their soul to killing pretty much everyone on Earth.

However, centuries later, Church leaders like Athenagoras spelled out in detail how demons like the spirits of the Nephilim attack people. It is quite different than just tempting them to worship idols. When people look at idols, which are all matter, they are basically contaminated with spirit of matter, which corrupts us. They attack the mind, and as a result people begin to think of evil things to do. Demons deposit delusion in our mind, and that is how they attack us.

What the Nephilim did—their murderousness, cannibalism, sexual assaults on animals—led to chaos on Earth, just as the Watchers' revealing various secrets to humans resulted in chaos. But in a sense, we can see ourselves as Nephilim. No, we don't practice cannibalism or have sex with animals, but we certainly engage in endless wars, rapaciously poison and destroy animals, and despoil the Earth; we even prey upon other human beings through oppression and exploitation, our versions of cannibalism. And not to put too fine a point on it, the societies we have built worship the idol of money.

The name of the Nephilim can be seen as connected to the concept of "fallen"—as in fallen angels—because the root of their name is said to mean "fall." Yet no mention of this is made in Second Temple Judaism, which is odd, because etymology is very important in Judaism. Some scholars make a distinction between the Nephilim and the Giborim, a word which is sometimes substituted for Nephilim. They identify the Giborim as straight-up giants that have nothing to do with the Watchers and the Nephilim as specifically the hybrid children of the Watchers and women. Enoch tells us that the Nephilim were destroyed; it's only 10 percent of their spirits who are allowed to survive the Flood specifically to lead humans into sin.

The Nephilim are referred to as "bastards" because they are not of Heaven or Earth. They are undefined and unlike anything else in the universe; this is why they are unclean. To me, this fits with a definite strand in Halakhah that forbids mixing of things that are ordinarily in separate categories, like milk and meat or linen and wool. Many people mock such separation, saying they are illogical or even laughable. It's not about logic or even about health. It's about ritual purity.

The Nephilim's great size seems to represent their voraciousness (and this is like our own rapaciousness with respect to the Earth and our own love affair with bigger and bigger things—bigger houses, bigger cars, larger servings of food, bigger lands, etc.). They are literally outside of divine order and neither they nor their actions fit into an orderly world. They also bear the violations perpetrated by their fathers against the divine order of the universe.

At around the same time that Athenagoras was ranking out women, *Pirqe di-Rabbi Eliezer* (around 830 CE) was describing how the wives of the Watchers gave birth as if to giant reptiles, bearing six children at a time—not just big births but huge ones. As soon as the Nephilim were born, they could walk and talk and prance around their parents like young lambs. They were **big**.

One thing to notice about the Nephilim, however, is their sterility. No female Nephilim seem to exist. They cannot have any children. As the progeny of two separate species, angels and humans, they are like mules, the progeny of horses and donkeys: sterile. This is a sort of sorrowful resonance of the reason why the Watchers wanted to go down to the women of earth in the first place: to have children. Their own children cannot fulfill this desire.

Giants vs. Nephilim

One fragment found at Qumran describes how the Giants who survived the Flood built the Tower of Babylon. They were scattered when the Tower was destroyed by God. Another fragment says that Abraham could trace his ancestors all the way back to the Giants that had been killed by God. One of them escaped, settled in Babylon, and built a tower as his home. It seems clear that these two fragments were written by two different people, and they certainly were not part of Enoch.

The short bit of Genesis that describes the Watchers event is interrupted by God talking about how human beings have a limited time to live; they are mortals, but angels are not. Angels can live forever. This implies that the Flood had to happen to destroy the Nephilim, who would have lived five hundred years or even forever otherwise. It is almost as if they have a relationship to Adam and Eve: recall that God had Adam and Eve ejected from the Garden before they could eat of the fruit of the Tree of Eternal Life.

Nevertheless, some people have believed that some of the Nephilim could have made it through the Flood by being members of Noah's family. They think we simply were not told that some survived. I think the latter is really reaching. Either it's part of the story that they survived or it isn't. In terms of them being part of Noah's family, this is dealt with in the part of Enoch that tells of Noah.

The Nephilim

There's a section of Numbers (13:33) that tells how the Israelites go to spy on the Anakites and come back terrified by their great size. They tell Moses that the Anakites were descended from the Nephilim and that's why they're so big. The spies are sure they could not possibly triumph over this giant people and the Israelites should go back to Egypt instead. But this notion is firmly trounced by God, who appears and complains about how the people have no faith and that their enemies will be destroyed, which is what happens. I am not so sure how much we should believe the spies when they compare the people of Canaan to giants. It sounds like just plain fear. Everyone's a giant when someone is scared of them.

In my opinion, there is a big difference between Nephilim and Giborim. Even when, occasionally, the two names are conflated in the Hebrew Bible, it's pretty clear that different groups are being discussed. The name of the Giborim is based on *gibor,* the word for "great, tall, mighty." That name fits the great heroes of old. The word Nephilim is apparently based on the word for "fall." That could not be more opposite than great, tall, mighty. The Nephilim are the children of the Watchers, who fell from their position as Holy Ones through their actions and fathered monsters.

CHAPTER THIRTEEN

Noah

Noah also fell, but he is not of the Nephilim. In the section of The Book of Enoch that describes Noah (chapter 106), we're told that when he was born, Noah was white and red, had white woolly hair, and his eyes lit up the room like the sun. As soon as he was born, he stood up in the midwife's hands and spoke blessings to God. His father, Lamech, was concerned and afraid that his son didn't look human. He worried that Noah might not be his own son at all, but some hybrid engendered by the angels. So he went to his father, Methuselah, to ask him to ask Enoch, Methuselah's father, whose child Noah was. We're not told how exactly Enoch contacts Methuselah, but it seems to be in trance.

Enoch tells Methuselah that Noah is really Lamech's son and that he will have the great task of helping his family survive the coming Flood. It seems to me very in keeping with stories the world over about people who were revered as saints that their birth and childhood was strange and compelling, that they were shining and precocious. This does not seem odd, and to some scholars it just is an indication of Noah's future role as divinely selected.

Some people have used this story as evidence that perhaps Noah had Nephilim ancestors or that there were Nephilim in his family. But remember that Noah is pictured as a white bull in The Animal Apocalypse, which means he is not considered one of the Nephilim or one of their descendants. In fact, we don't ever hear anywhere in Enoch that the Nephilim had any descendants. Also, the people who wrote Enoch would not have depicted the hero of the Flood as having the blood of Nephilim. They were the ones who were the *cause* of the Flood.

However, and this is a big however, consider an odd later story in the Hebrew Bible about Noah (Genesis 9:18–27). He became a farmer and was the first person to make wine. He drank it, got drunk, and passed out naked in his tent. His son Ham went in and saw him there and told his brothers, Shem and Japheth, who walked into the tent backwards and threw a cloak over their father to cover him. When Noah woke up, he knew what his "youngest son" had done to him and cursed Ham's son Canaan.

Why would he curse Ham's son? In Hebrew, the word used for "youngest son" can also mean "grandson," which Canaan was. Apparently, Canaan did more than just see his grandfather naked; he committed some kind of sexual assault on him. This is indicated by the choice of the Hebrew word for "uncovered" (there are four possible choices for that). The word chosen here is only used in relationship to sexual assault. It's not used to just mean "naked."

That's a pretty weird story, but what does it have to do with the Nephilim or any possibility of Nephilimism in Noah? First, there's the drunkenness, which implies a licentiousness to Noah's behavior. There is no commandment not to get drunk that I know of, but we all know that drunkenness can lead to violence of various sorts. In this case, it led to sexual licentiousness. Even though Noah didn't initiate or even consent to this sexual assault, he can be seen as somewhat responsible because he was passed out due to his own action and was therefore not able to prevent the assault. I know—this doesn't fit in with modern positions about sexual assault, but this is a very ancient text we are talking about, and they had different ideas about what constituted sexual assault.

For instance, when Lot's daughters despair of having a husband, they get Lot drunk so they can manipulate his genitals to provide semen to impregnate themselves (Genesis 19:30–37). This is not condemned. Why? Because they did it for what was considered a good reason: to have children in their ancestors' line. Also, their doing this very much adheres to the importance of trickery in Genesis. With Canaan and Noah, there would never be any children. There is nothing against sexual joy in the Hebrew Bible, but there is plenty against "wasting seed." Noah was wasting seed.

The drunkenness and the seed wasting might seem like Nephilim tendencies in Noah, but it doesn't make him one of the Nephilim. It does not even make him the descendant of Nephilim, but only a human being, like anyone. This contradicts the image of him we are shown in Enoch at his birth, but we all know that prodigies often are quite different people once they are grown.

In Jubilees, we learn that holy angels, not the Watchers, teach Noah how to work with plants spiritually to heal the sicknesses that demons or evil spirits are causing his children. This contrasts quite a bit with the root-cutting that the Watchers teach people and which is condemned. The difference is that holy angels teach Noah how to heal with plants, and we know that prayer to God is involved. There is nothing about harvesting these plants at propitious times according to the stars or exposing them to the night skies, as would be true for root-cutting.

To a certain extent, there is the implication that it is not the plants themselves that heal—that they are not actually physical medicine but just the placeholder for Noah's prayers and the blessings of the angels and the divine. So even though Noah is later held up as the first physician and first apothecary, he isn't acting as if the plants are medicinal. Still, it's an interesting opposition to the Watchers' shared knowledge of root-cutting, which is disparaged.

Noah

CHAPTER FOURTEEN

The Righteous

Some think that the Enochic writings are the product of or indicate a group of righteous people in Israel.[53] Enoch 10:16 refers to "the plant of righteousness and truth," and in the Apocalypse of Weeks (part of The Book of Enoch), we are told of "the chosen righteous from the chosen plant of righteousness." From these mentions, some conclude that an actual group was being referred to instead of a symbolic group. The scholar Boccaccini, who developed the idea of a body of literature and a form of Judaism called "Enochic," and some other researchers imagine that Enoch, or at least The Watchers, was read aloud to a group of people who were part of a sect, and that they responded to it aloud, as if for prayers or as part of a ritual. However, this group might be only some members of a community, a portion of a larger group, and not a sect on its own. The people in Qumran, who had made multiple copies of Enoch (which was written before their group was ever formed), seemed to use it to reinforce their own sense of community and righteousness, especially if we consider the critiques of the Temple priesthood. They envisioned a Temple not located on the land—not in Jerusalem but not in Tel Dan either—but instead in Heaven; that temple would include all the righteous of humanity.

Enoch puts forward a type of holiness that is similar to that of the angels and shows through the story that this level of spirituality can be reached by anyone, not just people who were descended from the approved lines of the priests of the Temple in Jerusalem. So even though some scholars believe that when the "chosen righteousness" or the "chosen plant of righteousness" is mentioned in Enoch, it is intended to mean a particular Jewish sect, we don't have any proof of that.

The Origin of Evil

One way to look at the origin of evil on Earth in Enoch is to see it as the incursion of foreigners. Evil comes not from people (Adam and Eve) but from completely non-human species like angels and the evil-minded half-breeds known as the Nephilim. Enoch doesn't even mention the contradiction between Adam and Eve's sin on the one hand and the Watchers' on the other.

But this idea of where evil came from was not popular in Second Temple Judaism even though Enoch was well known. For one thing, in Genesis, God wants to destroy everything in the world because of the sins of human beings and of all flesh. In Enoch, it's the Watchers and the Nephilim that God is angry with. That's quite a difference, and the Enoch version is not in keeping with the older version from Genesis.

You might have noticed that in Enoch, God is not paying attention to what is going on down on Earth. It's the four archangels, Michael, Sariel (elsewhere Phanuel is identified in this group instead), Raphael, and Gabriel, who hear the cries of the dead, and it's the archangels who criticize God for doing nothing. God is basically falling down on the job of being a judge and caring creator. At this point, we have not been told that human beings have not only been corrupted by the Watchers' teachings but are corrupting other people through those teachings. We don't get the same Genesis view of people just sinning all over the place and being so wicked that they are worthy of being destroyed. Instead, we're told how the Nephilim are mighty and eat up and kill everything on Earth and make war against each other. They could be compared to the ruling class. Some scholars have pointed this out, especially since later in Enoch, we hear about the mighty oppressing the righteous.

In terms of a rejection of Adam and Eve as the origin of sin on Earth, in Enoch we may notice that when Raphael shows Enoch the Garden of

Eden, nothing is said about the serpent, much less equating it with the Devil, nor about Adam and Eve breaking God's commandment that they not eat of the fruit of the Tree of the Knowledge of Good and Evil. We hear nothing about people gradually being separated from God but instead are told about an incident where evil was brought down to Earth by the residents of Heaven.

It's not until the first century CE that the first evil is situated not with the descent of the Watchers but with Adam and Eve. Not only is there less of a concentration on the Watchers and more on Adam and Eve and the Serpent but there is also less discussion of the Flood at that time. We see this shift also in sacred texts from that period, like 2 Baruch, written in the end of the first century CE or beginning of the second, which focuses on Adam as the source of death, grief, sickness, hard labor, pride, and more, all because of his sin of eating from the fruit of the Tree of Knowledge of Good and Evil.

We can then look at Enoch not being about the beginning of sin but about its end, when God will appear, the evil ones will be punished, the righteous will be treasured, and a new temple will arise. In fact, later readers will not believe that it was angels who brought evil to Earth but instead will see this work as being about how sins will be punished and God will sort things out.

As evidence, we see that the constant theme throughout Enoch is the punishment of wickedness. The people who read it might have seen the promise of a future righting of the world as both a blessing and a warning.

Mixing What Should Stay Separate

Sin is simply brought to exist on Earth because even if their intercourse with women was consensual, the Watchers violated a fundamental rule of ritual purity: things of different categories should not be mixed. According to Jewish law, which is comprised of commandments that occur in the Torah, there should be no mixing of wool with linen (animal-based textiles versus plant-based ones), no cooking a lamb in its mother's milk, priests can only marry women from priestly families, and so forth. It's all about keeping what should be separate (which is defined) as separate, about not mixing things that should not be mixed. For angels (who can't even have gender because they are spirits), not part of the animal kingdom, to have sex with humans is to mix things that should be kept separate (and even to mix their spirit with the flesh they must create to have sex with mortal beings). So even though there is no commandment anywhere among the 613 commandments mentioned in the Hebrew Bible that angels must not have intercourse with human beings, it is implied that it is a violation because it requires the mixing of categories that should not be mixed and that should remain separate for the sake of ritual purity.

The Nephilim are a mixture of two categories that should remain separate—angels and humans. That makes them transgressive by nature.

Angels have no need for sex, because sex is for beings who don't live forever. This is obliquely mentioned in the Genesis section referring to the Watchers' story. Since they have no need to reproduce, they shouldn't have engaged in sex with women. The perspective of Enoch is that sex is for making children, not fun. This is not the perspective of Judaism in general.

Mixing Is Okay in Heaven but Not on Earth

Mixing categories that should or must remain separate is wrong on Earth but it is fine in Heaven and even seems to be a characteristic of the place. Enoch sees Heaven, which is composed of layers of fire and snow, ice and lightning, hailstones and flames, and other things that in the material world remain separate and must do so for each to preserve their coherence. Enoch notices that there is no life there. This is an odd thing to say, in my opinion, until we think about all the laws that prohibit the mixing of categories in Judaism. Those laws are for the physical world and for human beings (life). I also take from this that the divine can combine these categories that we must hold separate—fire and ice don't destroy each other in Heaven—but on Earth they would both be destroyed. The Watchers combine things that should be separated—not only by having sex with women, which results in the destruction of many of the living things on Earth, including people, but the result of which is chaos. And in The Book of Enoch, sin is symbolized by chaos—so, for instance, the behavior of the Nephilim throwing off every bit of order to satisfy their appetites.

Further, the sharing on Earth of knowledge that the Watchers gained in Heaven is also a mixing of what should remain separate—heavenly knowledge and earthly knowledge. When heavenly knowledge is brought down to earth, it produces destructive hybrids—metalworking becomes arms manufacturing and tools of seduction. Chaos comes about due to this shifting of divine knowledge to earthly spheres, just as the destructive Nephilim result from the angels becoming flesh on Earth. That knowledge in the wrong place—or the wrong kind of knowledge—breeds monstrous behavior isn't much of a focus for people interpreting this book until later, but it seems built in to the worldview of Enoch.

Divine Order and the Chaos of Sin

Because Enoch is pious and righteous and follows divine order, it is not harmful for him to see and experience Heaven or the throne or even God, but those like the Watchers who have removed themselves from the divine order face destruction not only for the world (the Flood) and for their own children, but eventually for themselves. The Watchers in effect lose control over the ability to survive in a world of fire and ice, of mutually exclusive things that are destroyed when they are combined on Earth. They can't even return to Heaven, so great is their loss of the supernatural ability to tolerate the combination of opposites.

In contrast, Enoch, even though he is of Earth, of matter, can go into the palace made of tongues of fire and slabs of snow, where the ceiling is made of lightning. It is a house as hot as fire and as cold as ice, a place empty of life. In the throne room, which is an inferno, he looks upon the throne of the divine. It is made of ice with wheels like suns, and rivers of fire flow from beneath it. There is something extraordinary about him, as even the angels can't tolerate being close to the throne of God for too long—they will be burned up. Enoch has not become an angel, but he already has great angelic powers, and he can be alive in a place that he sees is otherwise empty of life.

The Righteous

A Critique of the Temple Priesthood

The scholar Boccaccini considers the Enoch story to be a metaphor—that the Watchers' descent from Heaven to bring evil to humans is really a retelling of how the priesthood of the Temple in Jerusalem was corrupted by foreigners, specifically, the Babylonians. One scholar points out that an indicator that the story is really about the Temple priesthood is the line in Enoch where the Watchers are told that instead of a human interceding for them in Heaven, they should be interceding for human beings. That would be the job of the Temple priesthood as well.

This corruption could have occurred through several means. If the Temple priests were having sex with menstruating women or prior to the required days to wait after it was over for sex to be ritually pure, then their children would be illegitimate and there goes the whole line of the priesthood after that person. Since the priesthood was a hereditary position, it's important that the chain of inheritance be unbroken.

Another possible source of ritual impurity would be that priests who were descended from those priests who had been captured and taken to Babylon might well have married Babylonian women who were of course not members of priestly families and might well not have even been Jews. This would be especially a problem when inheritance was through the maternal line, as it was in Judaism. The prophet Ezra commented about this issue when he visited Jerusalem and noticed that not only the ordinary elites but the priesthood and the Levites had foreign wives, thereby polluting the holy people.

Either way, if the priest is impure, then the sacrifices he offers to the divine on the behalf of the people are also impure and don't fulfill the commandments.

Ritual purity was a very important issue at Qumran, which might explain why there were multiple copies of Enoch found there; obviously Enoch was very popular with the people there. But other texts found there were also concerned with ritual purity. The people of Qumran saw their community as a kind of Temple substitute or alternative. They didn't set up a sacrificial cult of their own, but even while the Temple was still standing, some people were far more focused on study and prayers than on the sacrificial cult. If they thought the Temple was corrupted by the priesthood, they would see more value in staying away from it and using study and prayer instead. At the very least, the ritual purity they could attain at Qumran would be greater than they could acquire through the sacrificial cult because it was separated from the ritual impurity they might attach to the Temple of Jerusalem. And this is not even to touch upon any connections to the alternative Temple of the North.

Meanwhile, ordinary people had already been setting up alternative temples on high places that were in evidence during the time of the prophets, but these were seen by more sophisticated people as contaminated in a different way—by the influence of Canaanite (foreign) religion. For that matter, some even saw the temples of the North as having the same problem, although the worship of the Golden Calf at the center of those temples was not peculiar to the Canaanites but all over the entire Middle East. Even so, the area where those two northern temples were located is accorded a sacred status in Enoch, and it seems that whoever wrote at least parts of it went to the area of Dan and Hermon, and that these were places where visionary activity occurred.

We do have the sense that some of the people who wrote Enoch came from northern Galilee, where the temples of the North were located, and saw the Temple of Jerusalem as ritually impure. We must keep in mind, though, that it is not unusual for an ancient text to contain contradictions. It could be both for and against the temples of the North. Still, we know that nowhere in Enoch is the Temple of Jerusalem described as ritually pure. It is known, though, that the people of Qumran saw the Temple of Jerusalem as ritually impure and not legitimate, especially during the rulership of the Hasmonean priesthood. It would then appeal to them that Enoch describes a time when evil will come to an end. This would solve a multitude of problems for people who had issues with the Second Temple, not only those who wrote Enoch but the people of Qumran.

The Righteous

In Enoch, a new temple will arise and will not be dedicated to the sacrificial cult because sinning will be over and so no one will need to atone through sacrifice. This new temple will not be ritually impure and will not arise in Jerusalem, the entire city seen as polluted by the priests, but high above us. God will reside there, just as it was believed that God resided atop the Ark in the Temple in the past.

From this perspective, we can conclude that the problem in Enoch is not women or what they did or didn't do with the angels' teachings. Instead, it's about the power system of the Temple of Jerusalem and the great disagreements centered there over laws of purity and the importation of foreign practices, which are embodied in the Watchers' gifts. Enoch's writers lived in a very violent and tumultuous time, when the people were enduring fierce oppression. The idea of an era coming when God would destroy the oppressors and preserve the righteous people would have been very attractive to them but also clearly is favored even today.

Enoch might be put forward as a neutral voice in this matter because he is described as a scribe, not a priest or even a prophet. A scribe was learned and so would know what the law was but was not someone with power in the Temple hierarchy. Someone outside of the power framework might also mean they are outside of contamination or pollution, especially because being a scribe was not a hereditary position.

CHAPTER FIFTEEN

The Babylonian Exorcists

One scholar believes that the story of the Watchers was composed by Jews exiled to Babylonia. We don't have any evidence that this is true, but there are some intriguing parallels. For instance, Jewish exiles in Babylonia obtained jobs as temple scribes because, although the holy Babylonian texts were written in cuneiform on clay tablets and cuneiform was a difficult language that the exiles didn't know and that took years of training to learn, these texts and others were also transcribed into Aramaic and written on parchment and papyrus, which the Jewish exiles certainly did know. The Jewish Babylonian scribes didn't have the power of the exorcists. Those exorcists were messengers of the gods of exorcism, exorcising demons being one of their important jobs. Exorcism and illness were linked. But being able to read and copy the sacred Babylonian texts in Aramaic allowed the exiles a wide-open window into Babylonian religion, the religious power structure, and magical herbal medicine.

Some believe that foreign Jewish scribes saw that the Babylonian exorcists had certain bodies of knowledge and that instead of ridding people of demons, they called more demons into being through their ineptness. Their areas of expertise were very similar to what the Watchers taught humans. But I am not so sure that the similarity between what the Watchers taught and what the Babylonian exorcists knew was unique. I was struck right away by the similarity between what the Watchers taught and the original skill sets of alchemy, which didn't originate in Babylon or the Holy Land but in Egypt. It's also true that the astronomy of The Astronomical Book is not the Babylonian star system. That means there are some holes in this plot.

However, if the Watchers were based on the Babylonian exorcists, then it is as if Enoch is rejecting Babylonian culture and religion. We already know that the Prophets objected to Babylonian practices like astrology and the use of the lunar calendar in the Temple of Jerusalem, so it could also be that the critique of the Babylonian exorcists by way of the Watchers is only a guise for criticizing the priests of the Temple of Jerusalem. The Babylonian exorcists' practices of incorporating plants into exorcism has in the Watchers devolved into root-cutting, which is portrayed as if it were ordinary spellwork, like "make my lover come back to me," in order to belittle the practice.

The Babylonian exorcists used ritual and incantation texts. The lore of these texts was considered ancient by the Babylonians, written by Enki-Ea, the god of wisdom and exorcism. The Babylonian exorcists oversaw the treatment of illness in the Assyrian court by reading signs on the patient's body and by chanting incantations and administering plant remedies. They also visited the homes of sick people to predict whether the invalid would get well and who or what had sent the illness to the person. Particular symptoms indicated particular spirits. We can certainly see how this practice might be associated with the Watchers' teachings of root-cutting, astrology, and various types of the reading of signs. The Babylonian exorcists didn't incorporate straight-up divination into their medical practice, but they did advise people who were facing difficulty or considering risky ventures. The most important job of the Babylonian exorcists was to combat the udug/utukku, the prevalent Mesopotamian demon.

Sin Characterized by Chaos

Another perspective is that Enoch is really speaking to all the chaos that was occurring at the time it was written and is not in particular about the corruption of the priests or Babylon or anything else. In this worldview, sin leads to chaos, chaos leads to destruction, and destruction eventually leads to the restoration of purity and order. The most direct illustration of the link between sin and destruction is in chapters 6-11 of The Watchers.

We know no commandment forbids sex between angels and humans, so the Watchers needn't be condemned for that. God says the Watchers violated a divinely imposed and required order. I would elaborate on that to say that considering the great emphasis in the book is on the relationship between chaos and sin, that the big sin that the Watchers committed was not about sex with humans or even about teaching humans secrets or sharing "lesser" types of knowledge that resulted in bad doings. It's in their very name: they were Watchers, and they abandoned their posts in the stars to indulge themselves in pleasure. It was their divinely appointed job to guide the stars, and in return they lived in Heaven and were immortal.

They weren't forced to guide the stars; they chose not to. Or, from the perspective of another scholar, there was a covenant between God and the Watchers that they would guide the stars. This was not (and could not be) a Mosaic covenant or even a Noachide one; it was older. Breaking this covenant is why the stars (and the Watchers) are so severely punished. That's also why we periodically hear in Enoch about how the stars abandoned their official courses and how this causes havoc. Their job was not only divinely appointed but very important to the workings of the cosmos, yet they simply abandoned their posts for the sake of having fun, and in doing that, the world descended into chaos. Sin leads to chaos, and chaos leads to a destruction that only God can remedy.

We can interpret this in several ways with respect to why people used this book. We can say that it speaks to their own fear about the violence that surrounds them and that seems far beyond their control, as if it were being done by supernatural beings like horrifically blood-thirsty monsters. We can see it as a reprimand to those who are going against the law or the divine order and a warning to those on the slippery slope of transgression. We can see it as a promise to those who are oppressed that the people who are sinning and therefore creating chaos will eventually be punished. The godless will be destroyed and the righteous will attain eternal peace, certainly much to be wished for in troubled times.

The Babylonian Exorcists

The hope in the book is strongly represented, though, in the depiction of Enoch. This book offers those who follow the divine order and who are righteous the chance to rise bodily to Heaven, to look upon the divine throne, to see all sorts of far-flung places on Earth, to learn all kinds of secret knowledge, and to live forever. The reward of being pious is huge, and the punishment for rejecting divine order is also enormous.

We can also attach hope to the importance of ritual, for which ritual purity is important. Ritual is a way of maintaining order. Just as the stars appear at a certain time as part of the divine order, so the various holidays must be celebrated at the correct time, and if your calendar is a wonky mess, that's not going to happen. But there's more.

Because of the chaos in the divine order that is caused by the Watchers' sin, everything gets out of whack. The rain doesn't come at the right time, or there is less of it, and there will be drought. The plants make their seeds too late to germinate. Fruits can't ripen because they are produced too early or too late. The moon is too bright (which in other Jewish works is a sign of the end of time). Not only will people not understand the seasons or the travels of the celestial objects anymore, nature will disobey its own laws due to the transgressions that reflect disdain for God's creation. The stars won't move. This dire prediction gives human actions a lot of power over the forces of nature.

Two Kinds of Knowledge

Some knowledge is dangerous because it comes out of chaos—out of a straying from the divine order—and it seems that it becomes a carrier for chaos as if it were a virus. A curious parallel between the story of Adam of Eve and the story of the Watchers is how dangerous knowledge can be. People die because of it. Adam and Eve ate of the Tree of the Knowledge of Good and Evil, and for that were kicked out of the Garden and became mortal (and one of their sons ended up killing the other). If they had not gotten knowledge from the tree, they would have been immortal. In Enoch, knowledge of how to work metal and other gifts of the Watchers results in the death of almost the entire world.

The difference in knowledge depends on who has it. For instance, the Watchers teach sorcery and charms, root-cutting, metalworking, jewelry-making, how to make cosmetics including antimony eyeshadow (kohl), and divination through astrology, the sun, lightning, and the moon. We are told that these are all lesser forms of knowledge. But Enoch learns what are essentially magical oaths to control animals, healing; he is shown the mountains of metal, seven mountains of gems, and the mountain of antimony; he learns of the stars, the sun, the secrets of lightning, and lunar divination. It's clear that the value of a body of knowledge is not dependent on what the knowledge is but instead of the quality of the person who receives it—and where they got it from.

We might also say that there is a difference between knowledge in The Watchers and in Adam and Eve, but something we forget about the first couple is that if they had never gotten that knowledge, history would never have begun. Adam and Eve would have continued to live in the safe playpen of the Garden as God's cute little pets for eternity. They would never have become adults. Yes, the knowledge led to death, but it also led to life—and to freedom. Do we see this in Enoch?

In Enoch, the value of what anyone can know is dependent on how righteous they are. Enoch is often referred to as a teacher of righteousness or scribe of righteousness. Some semblance of freedom and the relationship to life occurs in Enoch in the contrast between "good" knowledge and "bad" knowledge. This is depicted in the book in a structural way. When the Watchers travel down to Earth, the knowledge they bring with them decreases in value; they literally go down and metaphorically the value of their knowledge decreases—it becomes contaminated and contaminating. Likewise, when Enoch rises to Heaven, the knowledge he receives, even though it is of the same fields as that of the Watchers' teachings, is increased. He literally goes up and the knowledge is likewise elevated.

But further, just as Adam and Eve attain freedom and new life by eating of the Tree of Knowledge of Good and Evil, so Noah and his children attain freedom from the predation of the Nephilim and a new life in a world that has been swept clean of monsters—or at least of most of them.

The Babylonian Exorcists

Also, Enoch attains life in the form of immortality as a resident of Heaven. We see that there are actually a lot of parallels between the story of the Watchers and the story of Adam and Eve. Maybe that's why the Watchers' story was eventually dropped; it became superfluous.

A good contrast between a good vs. an evil form of knowledge is found in writing. The Watchers taught writing that was considered evil because it referred to writing down oaths, and we are told that people should not be swearing out oaths because doing so implies a lack of trust. Angels also shouldn't be writing down things they are doing; only inferior beings do that. It is the equivalent of learning metalworking to make weapons of war instead of tools for farming. Enoch learned writing and instead of using it to write down oaths, wrote about the order of the seasons, about weeks, and wrote a testimony for his children.

The Watchers' Teachings

No "forbidden teachings" are mentioned in the Watchers' section of Genesis; in fact, no teachings are mentioned at all. In the Hebrew Bible, at least one of the bodies of forbidden knowledge that Enoch mentions as the Watchers sharing with human beings had already been invented by the sons of Cain—metalworking (they also invented cities, cattle herding, and music). In various parts of the Mediterranean, metallurgy, divination, and pharmacology are linked in myth, so it's not strange to see them together here. In Aramaic myths, that group of skills included reading the stars, lightning, actions of the Earth, the moon, and the sun as part of divination; the ancient Greeks focused more on astrology. To me, reading the signs of lightning is most interesting. Root-cutting was also a part of ancient Greek magic as well as a version in Babylonian exorcism.

The secret knowledge that the Watchers share falls into three groups: cultural arts like metalworking and human ornamentation, magic such as spells and root-cutting, and divination through the reading of celestial bodies and weather. At least one scholar has argued that the first category has to do with the Noachide commandments, which apply to Gentiles (anyone who is not Jewish). These were given by God to Noah and his children, who represent all humankind, and acted as a covenant. As long as people observed these laws, God promised not to send another Flood. This covenant is symbolized by the rainbow.

These laws were seven (six negative and one positive): 1) no worship of idols, 2) no cursing God, 3) no killing, 4) no sex outside of marriage (although premarital sex is okay if it leads to marriage) and no male homosexuality, 5) no stealing, 6) no cutting flesh from a living animal, and 7) courts of justice must be established.

By the way, the "homosexuality" here can mean two separate things: "Men, don't have anal sex with another man" (so other kinds of sex between men are okay) or "Men, don't have sex with a man who belongs to a woman" (make sure he's single). The phrasing is unique and thus ambiguous. There is no forbidding of lesbian sex at all.

We can see how metalworking and creating human ornamentation (jewelry, makeup, dyeing clothing) could comprise violations of about half of these commandments—against killing due to weapons being made, ornamentation leading to sex outside of marriage, and metalworking abilities also perhaps tied to making idols and things like amulets.

Secrets Unjustly Revealed

In chapters 9 and 10 of Enoch, we begin to see the mention of the theme of secrets that the Watchers unjustly revealed; this is described as one of the main reasons why they were punished. We read, for instance, of the four archangels discussing how wrong it was for the Watchers to reveal these things. One of the arts the archangels mention is divination, but recall that Daniel praises Enoch as a diviner in the courts of foreign kings. So how wrong can divination be? We also see how in other sections, Enoch encourages people to study the stars, the moon, the sun, and so forth to learn the divine orderliness of the universe. The thing is that I doubt that the people the Watchers taught used that secret knowledge to learn the divine orderliness of the universe. I think they had other uses in mind.

Despite biblical prohibition of some types of magic, ordinary Jews practiced magic from ancient times, and many made their living from it.

They didn't live in fear of being discovered or excommunicated or put in jail. On the contrary, people were magicians for hire and communities had official magic workers. Today, among Jews who believe in magic, many feel that it was okay for the Sages to practice it, but not for us, which reminds me of the division between Enoch and the fallen Watchers and how their otherwise identical practices are judged. Still, other modern Jews consider magic to be fine and consult professional amulet-makers, etc.

To some extent, the practice of magic is often condemned because the magical practitioner is incapable of doing it, despite their claims. They are then thought to be incompetent at best and frauds at worst. Let's look at Daniel, since that book was written around the same time as Enoch and outright features divination. The court magicians in Daniel not only interpret dreams but do magic to change them and to effect the future the dream predicts. These professional magicians are not condemned in Daniel for doing magic; they are condemned for being incompetent. They can't interpret the king's dreams. Daniel says that he can do so because God reveals secrets (by the way, he does not say that the court magicians' wisdom comes from demons). Basically, the court magicians are not called evil, just lame.

We might compare this criticism to that of the Babylonian exorcists, if we decide that Enoch is about attacking or mocking them. We could see that kind of mockery coming out of nationalism. However, the priests of the Temple of Jerusalem are another story. It seems they are not just incompetent but sinners, plain and simple.

At least one author believes the part about the Watchers teaching secrets was added later. Some argue that the people who wrote Enoch used the story of the Watchers because it suited their purposes (remember that the essence of the story doesn't mention Enoch; it's clearly from somewhere else). It seems that the part about the Watchers' teachings was added to increase Enoch's reputation as a sage, especially when his knowledge, which is divine and given freely, is contrasted to the Watchers' knowledge stolen from a place they can no longer enter. The other thing is that the writers had a strong interest in astronomy and astrology, so a story about the angels who previously guided the stars and brought a lot of star-based (and other) divination methods down to Earth would be of interest to them.

It is not strange to say that it was not what the Watchers taught but the fact that it was stolen and used for ill purposes (like war) that was important to the writers of Enoch. The wrong was not within the knowledge itself. In fact, the whole thing of transmitting forbidden knowledge is only very rarely a part of pre-Rabbinic texts and the teaching of this knowledge is not mentioned in Second Temple Jewish sources or in Christian Scriptures. Both Jews and Christians initially ignored the illicit instruction aspect of Enoch.

The secrecy is at the heart of what is wrong about the Watchers' teachings, not the subjects. Later, Ben Sira wrote: "Seek not what is too difficult for you,/ Nor investigate what is beyond your power. Reflect on what has been assigned to you,/ For you do not need hidden things." (Sirach 3:21–22)

Everyone should stay in their own lane, as far as Ben Sira is concerned.

The secret knowledge that Enoch learns is different from what the Watchers teach because their knowledge helped to tear the Earth apart and deform nature itself, and Enoch's knowledge was intended to heal the Earth. In other words, the Watchers' knowledge brings chaos and Enoch's knowledge will bring order.

The first time spilling forbidden knowledge or secrets is mentioned, it is shared with the wives only (7:1). Later, it's shared with everyone. So it's certainly not only the wives who are to blame; everyone gets hold of the secrets, and many of them are used to a bad purpose. I wonder if that's because even within this text, while the center is about how heavenly beings brought evil to Earth, the writers hedged their bets and depicted a world full of people ripe for transgressing.

The Babylonian Exorcists

CHAPTER SIXTEEN

Christian Responses to the Watchers' Teachings: Women Are Evil

Generally, other texts that referred to The Watchers rarely said that the Watchers' teachings were corrupting; they hardly even mentioned the teachings at all, until Christianity became the dominant religion.

Both Tertullian and Cyprian use the Watchers' teachings and their results as a "proof" that women should not be allowed to wear jewelry or makeup. Tertullian even believed that evil is empowered in the world due to the weakness of women; to choose makeup is to choose the demonic. For him, makeup is literally the product of demons. He argues that women were the ones who were making cosmetics and jewelry that they used as a weapon to cause men to sin. He was familiar with Enoch but modified the text to suit his own misogyny. He shifts the focus away from the sin of all human beings (with a few exceptions, like Noah) to the sin of women. We can easily see how Eve becomes the model of a wheedling devil who seduces poor dumb Adam into eating the fruit of the Tree of the Knowledge of Good and Evil. Women don't even have any need to learn magic; they can just gussy themselves up and not only are they then able to con the angels down from Heaven, but they can cause the destruction of the entire world. It is difficult to stomach the depth of Tertullian's hatred for women.

Cyprian, who was much influenced by Tertullian, is not far behind in terms of his misogyny. In his work *On the Dress of Virgins*, he writes as if the Watchers' teachings were only given to women. For that reason and because he sees women as so weak and so evil, he basically ignores what the

Watchers did by rejecting their assigned task of being steadfast guides of the stars and instead coming down to Earth to have sex instead and father a generation of monsters who set about killing the world.

Both Tertullian and Cyprian use the bad effect of the Watchers' teachings on women to argue that women should not be allowed to adorn themselves at all. Somehow the making of the weapons of war is simply glossed over and we are left with the ridiculous estimation of makeup being worse than swords.

The transgressiveness of the Watchers' teachings has a lot in common with the commandments against breaking of the mixing rule; the problem is not that they taught sorcery, for instance, but that this practice was meant to stay in Heaven and not be spread around on Earth—the sin was mixing the practices of Heaven with those of Earth. In other words, it is knowledge out of context when it is brought down to earth. If angels were studying and using it up in Heaven (and apparently, they were, for how else would they have learned it), that would be okay. To bring it out of that space and cause it to germinate all over the world is the big problem.

As much as Tertullian, Cyprian, and other Christians would argue that the Watchers' real wrong came from sharing secret knowledge with their wives, the fact is that the Watchers shared them with both men and women (Enoch 16:3).

Some have argued that the knowledge that the Watchers shared with the wives was somehow second-rate, inferior, and contaminating. There is the contrast between the secrets that the Watchers took down to Earth with them, stealing them from Heaven and bringing them to an unholy, impure place like Earth. We might consider that it's exactly the bringing down that causes the secrets to become "rejected" mysteries, that the secrets are defiled by the process of bringing them down (much as the Watchers are themselves contaminated and no longer allowed back into Heaven because they went down to Earth and had sex there).

We might also consider that the wrong the Watchers did was the betrayal of a trust, and what's more, a divine trust. They were shown these secrets up in Heaven because they were angels, and they betrayed that trust

144   The Forbidden Knowledge of The Book of Enoch

by sharing them with their new human wives as if these divine secrets were pillow-talk. They were supposed to keep this knowledge secret and instead they released it into the world so that not only could non-angels use it, but it could furthermore then be perverted as the knowledge of making agricultural implements was turned to making weapons of destruction.

As with any ancient text (a good example is the Hebrew Bible), if you don't know the language the text was written in, and know it well, you are at the mercy of the translator. It's not unusual for translators to tweak the translation in a direction they feel it should go, maybe without even meaning to, or due to a simple lack of sufficient knowledge. The Greek translations of Enoch tell us that the angels knew heavenly secrets and revealed them to human beings, but in the Ethiopic translations, the Watchers transmit secret knowledge that was corrupted before they got their hands on it. The thing is that if the forbidden knowledge they shared was false, then they aren't as guilty of a transgression as they would be if it were true knowledge.

To some extent, the assertion that the Watchers should be condemned because they shared true knowledge that should have been kept secret reminds me of discussions about whether plans to make an atomic bomb, or how to manufacture meth, or how to use poisonous plants for various non-lethal purposes should be shared online. As a teacher, I believe that releasing true information to the wild is important. For one thing, any body of knowledge requires not only learning about a topic but getting off one's ass and doing the work to actually use it, and that means developing a specific set of real-world skills instead of just brain work. Knowledge doesn't turn into action without practice.

A knife may be used to cut bread or to stab someone to death. It's the same knife. Knowledge is not deadly. It's what we do with it that is. I think the best example of that is right in Enoch, with the skill of metalworking. There was nothing wrong with teaching people metalworking. There was something wrong with using that skill to make swords, shields, and chain-mail instead of plows, hoes, and horseshoes. It's sort of like using one's knowledge of fireworks to make a bomb. It's not the knowledge that is to blame; it's how it's used. And just like learning to use fireworks, any sort of magical practice, such as binding spells, can blow up in your face. That is not the fault of the knowledge. It's an operator error.

If we do want to examine whether there is true or false forbidden knowledge, we can look at how the skills the Watchers taught were also taught by angels to Enoch, for example, herbal medicine vs. root cutting. In Jubilees, which takes part in Enoch's worldview, we hear how Noah was taught how to use plants to cure sickness and "seductions" that his children acquired due to the actions of the evil spirits that came out of the bodies of the Nephilim. We know that root-cutting involved not only healing people possessed or attacked by demons but that it was empowered by the herbs being harvested at particular times and in particular ways as well as being exposed to the stars.

How was Noah's herbalism different? He first prayed to God that his children be healed, and he was then given the knowledge of the herbs. But it is made clear to us that it is not the herbs themselves that heal his children; the herbs are empowered by his prayers. Further, the herbs are protective rather than acting like a medicine; they treat disease by repelling evil. He gave strength to the herbs through prayer instead of gathering energy for them from the stars.

One scholar has mentioned that the very fact that Noah is depicted as mastering using herbs to heal illnesses caused by demons, exactly what the Babylonian exorcists did, was a means for transferring traditions from Babylon to Israel and modifying and elevating those traditions by redirecting their center of power from the stars to the God of Israel. Jubilees posits that the real difference between these two very similar bodies of knowledge regarding herbs has much to do with where the operator gets their power—from spirits as undependable as the Watchers turned out to be (remember, they were captains of the stars) or from angels who were steadfast. One scholar has pointed out that the author(s) of Jubilees thought this type of herbalism had value, where apparently the authors of Enoch did not. Sorcery and spellwork are bundled with root-cutting in Enoch.

146   The Forbidden Knowledge of The Book of Enoch

Still, it isn't clear that the root-cutting taught by the Watchers was used only for negative purposes.

Enoch's possible suspiciousness of herbal medicine might come because of the ancient idea that illness is a divine punishment. For instance, there's the story of how the Prophet Miriam and the priest Aaron were criticizing Moses for marrying a foreigner (Numbers 12). Miriam and Aaron compare themselves to Moses in terms of their ability to prophesy, and God hears them and gets mad. He appears to them in a cloud and says that Moses is different from them, because God appears to prophets through dreams and visions, but to Moses, God has appeared face to face. The implication of course is that Moses is above other prophets. When Aaron and Miriam leave the tent, Miriam is struck with leprosy. (For some reason, nothing happens to Aaron, but frankly whatever happened to him seems to have been edited out to establish the line of Aaron as the pure priestly line.) Aaron begs Moses to ask God to cure her, and Moses prays to God for that. God tells them that Miriam must be removed from the people in a tent separate from the camp for seven days, after which time she can come back—and the implication is that then she will be healed.

Since leprosy was a disease that made people ritually impure among the Israelites, giving it to Miriam completely undercut her position as a prophet. It was a serious punishment. We can see here how illness was used as a punishment in the Hebrew Bible, and in that case, trying to cure the person with medicine would not be praiseworthy. The ill could only be cured by divine intervention brought about by prayer.

However, once the Temple was built, one job of the priests was to guard ritual purity and watch out for ritual impurity. They were not healers, but they did decide who was ritually impure or ritually pure. In Jubilees, Noah is in place of the priests; his sons come to ask his help when their own sons begin to fall ill due to demonic attack (Jubilees 10:1).

There are also various examples of virtuous people having exceedingly good health and living to extreme old age in the Hebrew Bible; healthy old age is the reward of righteousness. Clearly, righteous people in that view would never need medicine of any kind, so there's a subtle implication that physical illness is due to spiritual illness like sin.

The Babylonian practice of root-cutting meant that herbs were harvested only at certain times, like when the sun was down. The exorcist would cut the plant with their head covered and might draw a circle of protection around the plant. These plants were then exposed to starlight. Diseases might be caused not just by evil spirits/demons but by ghosts/the spirits of the dead.

Root-cutters typically sold the herbs to physicians and to medicine sellers. It was a secret knowledge, bringing to my mind blacksmithy, with its occult knowledge of herbal quenches. Just so, the herbs had to be harvested at certain times, outside of when they might be most potent biologically, such as before flowering—directions might include harvesting in the dark, or under certain stars, and many of the practices that come down to the notes made by naturalists of the Edwardian period repeat the type of mini rituals that were commonly a part of root-cutting.

Foreigners Are the Problem

There is a valid argument to be made that the Watchers don't represent Babylonian exorcists or priests of the Temple of Jerusalem but simply foreigners. Around the time that The Watchers, the core of Enoch, was written, the Land of Israel was invaded by the Diadochi (323–302 BCE) and was later under the control of the Seleucids (217–198 BCE), with the result that in twenty-one years, the area changed hands at least twenty-one times. You can imagine the violence and deprivation the Israelites must have experienced at the hands of these outsiders.

The Diadochi in the past were said to have been the target of Enoch, because some claimed that they were descended from deities. From this perspective, Enoch might be interpreted as a satire; the ancestors of the Diadochi were then comparable to Watchers, spirits who disobeyed God and went on to father broods of destructive, murderous hybrid entities who destroyed the Earth. Not much divine about that. The problem is that there is almost no evidence that the Diadochi ever said such things about themselves, so the idea that Enoch satirizes them has been abandoned. However, it should be said that there was plenty of mockery and satire in ancient texts.

We can see how the Prophets such as Isaiah, who lived through times of violence and foreign oppression, responded to oppressors like the Diadochi or Antiochus. Isaiah is known for asking when God will react, like how the souls of the dead wail to Heaven in Enoch but God does nothing until the archangels nag him. The big difference, however, is that in Isaiah, there is no talk of spirits oppressing people, but instead other humans are the oppressors. Daniel 10-12 features a viciously oppressive foreigner, Antiochus Epiphanes, who is depicted as basically the antithesis of God.

In other words, we have a history of sacred figures calling out to God for vengeance and praying to God to take action to right the wrongs committed by foreign oppressors.

Who's Guilty?

The Book of Enoch is itself slippery in terms of whether the Watchers are responsible for the defiling of the Earth or if humans are. To a great extent, who's responsible for what depends on the translation you are reading. A modern scholar, for instance, uses a translation made by Syncellus to say that Asael taught men how to work metal for war but also how to make bracelets and ornaments, dyes, eyeshadow, and so forth for themselves and for women, and it was this that led the holy ones into sin.

This does mean that at least as far as that translation is concerned, there were two different ways that evil arose on Earth. But we also have to remember that, as mentioned before, ancient texts are often contradictory, and this was not seen as a fault. It does leave the text more open to interpretation and it denies us any ultimate Truth. Instead, we are forced to choose a plot point and see where it leads in terms of spirituality or ethics.

But even if we gloss over the differences in translations, we still have a secondary story in The Animal Apocalypse where one star falls from Heaven and then is joined by a bunch of other stars (Enoch 86:1–2). Some consider that this means that the Asael story was older.

Christian Responses to the Watchers' Teachings: Women Are Evil

Many Jews and Christians focused on the angels' sexual misdeeds, but some zero in on the teachings. You can read it from the order it appears in the text and say that the teaching happened because of the sexual stuff, kind of like an outgrowth. Others see Asael's work as why Shemihazah's group came down to earth—they were tempted by the products of Asael's work, the jewelry, etc. Or that even Asael taught first before any sexual stuff happened, and that the sexual happened precisely because of what Asael taught. It's not surprising, then, that the Earth is partly healed when Asael is put into the ground in Enoch 10:7.

Reversals and Oppositions

A characteristic of Enoch is its use of various reversals. For instance, the Watchers, who were among the stars and guiding them, drop down to Earth to have sex with women. This descent is matched with a drop in their power and respectability—they can no longer return to Heaven or stand in the presence of the divine, and their power is obviously seriously lessened because they can be imprisoned in holes in rocks.

There's also the contrast of opposites, as mentioned. Almost every subject that the Watchers teach is also something that Enoch learns, but the subjects he is taught are from an elevated source. Here we are shown two types of revelation: improper (Ch. 6–11) and proper (Ch. 17–36). And as the Watchers are no longer elevated beings, some readers think the subjects they teach can be seen as corrupted.

Another reversal is that the archangels ask Enoch to go scold the Watchers for what they've done and what has been unleashed by their actions, but the Watchers ask Enoch to intercede with Heaven on their behalf. One request asks him to descend and scold, and the other calls for him to ascend and plead.

A perhaps unnoticed opposition is how the archangels focus on what the angels did wrong by leaving Heaven and by their progeny, the Nephilim. In contrast, Enoch zeroes in on the people and the sins they learned from Asael.

PART THREE

OTHER ENOCHIC WORKS

CHAPTER SEVENTEEN

The Book of Jubilees

Jubilees was written in the Hasmonean period, in the second century BCE, probably between 170 and 150 BCE, and is very much associated with Enoch. The big difference between how Jubilees tells the Watchers' story and how Enoch tells it is that Jubilees is not about explaining how evil came into the world, which is one task Enoch accomplishes. Instead, Jubilees is about the necessity of observing the commandments and the punishment awaiting those who don't. Mosaic Law is of vital importance to Jubilees, whereas for Enoch, neither Mosaic Law nor the covenant are mentioned. Instead, the transgression is against divine order.

Scholars believe that the author of Jubilees knew The Watchers, and some see Jubilees as a partner to Enoch. They also say that the Aramaic Levi Document was probably the source for Jubilees. It uses the same 360-day calendar. That text was written in the third or early second century BCE, while Jubilees was written in the second century BCE, so although the authors of Jubilees did not have the complete Enoch, they certainly had access to The Astronomical Book and The Watchers. Jubilees tells the stories of the Hebrew Bible from Genesis 6:1–4 (the Watchers story) through Exodus 6–16 (ending with the Israelites receiving manna in the desert) and draws on not only the Pentateuch but other Enochic books and oral Biblical interpretation.

The book considers that Enoch first told people what a jubilee was: forty-nine years (it seems clear that this is an oblique reference to a solar calendar (52 weeks or 7 days × 52 weeks = 364 + 1 extra day) rather than a lunar calendar (thirteen months plus a leap month every two to three years). In turn, the book tells of forty-nine jubilees plus one. Forty-nine is seven times seven, and among the Israelites (and many other cultures), seven was a very important number—probably because they considered that there were seven visible "planets": Sun, Moon, Mercury, Venus, Mars, Saturn, and Jupiter.

The Watchers don't come down to Earth to have sex with women in Jubilees. Instead, God sends them to teach humans how to do what is just and right, and at no point does Jubilees criticize their teachings. However, once they get to Earth, their mission goes out the window because they are weak and disobedient. I believe the reason why this mission was created for the Watchers in the Jubilees plot line is because it excuses Heaven from being the origin of evil.

When the Watchers had sex with women, the angels became unclean. This isn't the same as 'sinning in Jubilees' worldview. Instead, it's ritual impurity. Further, the fact that they had sex with women was not what made the Watchers ritually impure; instead, it was the fact that they had sex with women who were menstruating. In a way, this version of the Watchers is closer to the story of Adam and Eve, which is retold at the beginning of Jubilees, so the assurance is there in the book that the Watchers did not bring evil to Earth; it was already there, made by human beings. Once the Watchers have sex with women, the plot follows the Shemihazah story.

Unlike in Enoch, from which Moses and Mount Sinai are absent, Moses is an important character in this book. But he functions mainly as a witness to the traditions of Enochic texts, thus building their importance. Jubilees tries to balance Moses and Enoch. Jubilees makes the point that revelation didn't occur only at Mount Sinai. It occurred with Enoch. Also, in this work, we don't see Moses receiving the Law from YHVH on Mount Sinai. Instead, he receives Jubilees from an "angel of the presence" on Mount Sinai. This phrase is often used to identify Metatron, but that angel does not appear in Enoch, only in the later Enochic writings. Some later interpreters conflate Metatron with Enoch, but some scholars reject this interpretation.

Enoch and Jubilees have much in common with Mesopotamian traditions. They share the idea that the great revelations occurred at the beginning of history and were followed by the destruction of the Flood, which divides mythical time from legendary time. Historically, it was common to say that the foundational events of history occurred in some primeval time, so Enochic literature shares that aspect with Mesopotamian stories. To instead switch primeval events to a mountain in the middle of the desert in historical time, as the Hebrew Bible did, was completely unique.

One difference between Enoch and Jubilees is that in Enoch, most humans have been killed, primarily by the Nephilim, but in Jubilees, humans have been engaged in bloodshed and violence along with the Nephilim. The destruction that the Flood will bring is for every human except Noah and his family.

Shemihazah and Asael are not mentioned in Jubilees, even though it borrows the plot from Enoch. In Jubilees, the Watchers are incarcerated and the Nephilim are destroyed, but a ton of demons and evil spirits, whom Jubilees identifies as children of the Watchers (Jubilees 10:15), are left to bedevil the world after the Flood. The head of these evil spirits is named Mastema, whose name means "hostility." His job is to manipulate people into committing sins like eating blood, and he will send evil spirits to lead them into the worship of idols. This means that human sin comes from demonic activity. We might see Enoch as shifting the origin of evil from humans to angels, but Jubilees shifts the persistence of evil to demons acting on humans.

Mastema can do more than order spirits around, however. He can also cause what seems like natural disasters. While Abraham is still in Ur, the city where his family originated, Mastema sends birds to eat seed that has just been sown in the fields, and a famine results (Jubilees 11:11–24).

At one point, Abraham has learned astrology and is sitting outside at night looking at the stars and trying to read what might occur in the

The Book of Jubilees

coming year. He decides that there is no reason for him to read the stars when he could just ask God.

The implication in Jubilees is that books about astrology are demonic. We see this in the depiction of Cainan (Jubilees 8:2–4). He lived after Abraham and before Noah. He uses the Hebrew his father taught him to read an inscription he finds on a stone; the implication is that the information written there is ancient. This explains how the forbidden knowledge that was revealed before the Flood persisted and continued to influence people even after most were destroyed. From that writing Cainan learned astrological divination, which was one of the teachings of the Watchers. This includes reading the signs of the sun, moon, stars, and the weather.

The inappropriate sex partner issue comes up in Cainan's story. After he has found the writing on the rock, translates it, and acquires the forbidden knowledge of astrology, Cainan goes on to find a wife outside of the house of Shem. He instead chooses a wife from the house of Japheth, who is the father of the Greeks (Jubilees 8:5). We see that forbidden knowledge is sturdy enough in its corrupting evil to survive the death and disappearance of the Watchers and, like a virus, infect people who use it so that they open themselves to foreigners and thus to a lifetime of ritual impurity for themselves and their family. Cainan is an example of someone other than the Watchers' wives or other women learning forbidden knowledge.

Women are not blamed for seducing the Watchers in Jubilees either. The angels succumb to their own lust because they are weak.

Enoch is a bit different in Jubilees—he has much more influence on the world in general. He learned how to read and write Hebrew from the angels and wrote about which constellations are visible during each of the months. He wrote about the calendar and everything else that he was taught by the angels, with whom he lived for six jubilees.

Another difference is that Jubilees was written in Hebrew and Enoch was written in Aramaic. Why did the person who wrote Jubilees choose Hebrew? Because not only was the choice of Hebrew a nationalist choice— it was not learned in Babylon, it was the language of the Hebrew people— but Hebrew already had the power of esoteric speech. In a sense, it is itself a secret knowledge. It is depicted as being learned through the aid of angels and is therefore a closed practice. And since in the Hebrew Bible, the universe was created by God speaking in Hebrew, it has enormous magical power.

In Jubilees, we learn that God decided to reveal Hebrew to Abraham, who first spoke Hebrew with an angel and could understand the texts of his ancestors only if the angel helped him. This is a good example of how Hebrew is depicted as a tool of supernatural knowledge in this book.

In Enoch, we hear how the Watchers teach people root-cutting. In Jubilees 10:1–14, we hear how Noah's five sons come to him for help. Demons commanded by Mastema are tormenting Noah's grandsons, misleading them and manipulating them into behaving stupidly (Jubilees 10:1). They are blinding and killing the grandsons.

Noah prays to God and tells God about these events, reminding God how God protected him and his family during the Flood. He asks God to be merciful once more so that his children and grandchildren could fill the Earth. Noah reminds God of the Watchers and says these savage, evil spirits are the Watchers' children and that they made humans sin prior to the Flood. He asks God to imprison the evil spirits who've remained alive so they can't torment his progeny anymore. It is the combination of prayer and herbs, the use of which has been taught to him by holy angels, that helps Noah treat their diseases.

God tells the angels to bind the evil spirits, but Mastema intercedes and asks that some of the evil spirits be allowed to remain under his command. Mastema says that the spirits were there precisely to cause destruction and to misdirect people as a way of punishing human beings for being evil. He argued that the spirits should be preserved for this task. God thought he was right and allowed him to keep one-tenth of the evil spirits for his purposes. However, he also told the holy angels to teach Noah how to make medicine against the illnesses that the demons cause. Noah wrote this all down in a book.

Mastema plays a role like that of the opposer (*satan*) in Job. He incites God to test Abraham by asking him to sacrifice his son Isaac. Mastema is

The Book of Jubilees

scolded when it turns out that Abraham is so faithful to God that he is willing to sacrifice his son.

However, the tenth of the demons that remained were still destructive and they spread forbidden knowledge. Jubilees puts forward the central idea that the world is a battle between good and evil spirits, and this battle characterizes entire nations as one or the other. Although demons lead people to worship idols, they don't actually inhabit idols themselves. Idols are dead and empty in the worldview of Jubilees.

Jubilees has a different take on forbidden knowledge. The Nephilim were taught it by the Watchers and they use it to destroy people.

In The Watchers and Giants, God destroys the Earth with the Flood because of the sins of the Watchers and the Nephilim. In Jubilees, the Flood is the punishment for human behaviors that they learned because of the Watchers' actions.

Mount Sinai is fundamentally important to Jubilees, since the book's action begins and ends there. That's where an angel of the presence (who might be Enoch himself) talks to Moses.

There is a focus in Jubilees on keeping the Sabbath, but by that means we know it was not created by the Essenes, since that was not a major concern for them.

Jubilees connects Jacob, who is an important character in the book, with Enoch. According to Jubilees, Enoch wrote down what was revealed to him in seven tablets. An angel shows these tablets to Jacob, and he copies them and gives them to his son Levi. Here we see an example of a transmission of good knowledge as opposed to the transmission of bad knowledge that Cainan finds inscribed on a rock (literally from the dead).

Jubilees and Mosaic Law

The people of Qumran mentioned two sets of laws in their Rule of the Community: there were *niglot*, laws that had been revealed in the Pentateuch, and *nistarot*, laws that were hidden in Pentateuch and only revealed by members of the sect through interpretation of the Bible. The idea of hidden laws occurs in The Damascus Document with respect to the Sabbaths and the Festivals. Qumran was not very taken with Biblical (Mosaic) law.

Jewish Hellenists regarded the law of Moses as problematic because it caused Jews and Gentiles to be separate from each other, which in turn resulted in friction between them. They argued that before Mosaic law, Jews and Gentiles got along just fine (although there is no historical evidence for this peaceable condition). They especially didn't like circumcision and *kashrut* (ritual purity with respect to food, such as not eating certain animals and slaughtering in a particular way the ones that are considered pure enough to eat). Such practices didn't fit in with what Hellenized Jews thought of as a universal religion. The conclusion among Hellenistic Jews was that Mosaic law should be modified. The Maccabees fought against this; they wanted Mosaic law to be stronger and more widely observed as a matter of national identity. But Jubilees argues that Mosaic law always existed, before Moses, and the ancestors followed these laws even before Moses was born. Jubilees is very anti-Gentile, mostly because they worship idols, which in this context means they succumb to demons. It's all the more interesting, then, that in Jubilees Moses receives Jubilees, not the Ten Commandments.

Jubilees posits that at the end of time, the Israelites will return to their home in the Land of Israel, which was given to them after the Flood, and which was taken from them by the Canaanites, who are descended from Ham (remember, this is not a history book). At that time, the Israelites will all be purified.

Enoch talks some about injustice and the oppressors of the people, but Jubilees makes injustice one of three evils that the Watchers brought with them, and that people should avoid: sexual transgressions, ritual impurity, and injustice; we can definitely see the relationship here to Noachide law. In Jubilees, injustice has come about because of all the violence perpetrated by the Watchers' children. The only way this can be defeated is for the Israelites to live separately from Gentiles and especially not to have sex with them. This is completely opposed to the views of Hellenistic Jews.

The Book of Jubilees   **159**

CHAPTER EIGHTEEN

The Rape of Dinah

The Rape of Dinah is first told in Genesis in a fairly detailed way. This story is retold in Jubilees in a shorter and less nuanced form and is used as an argument against intermarriage (and it is very resonant with the story of the Watchers: have sex with foreigners and your world will be destroyed).

Jacob and his family are residing in Shechem, whose prince of the same name kidnaps and rapes Jacob's daughter Dinah. The language in the story makes it clear that Dinah is taken and raped; this is not one of those occasions where in ancient texts a couple runs off together and must put forward the fiction that the woman has been kidnapped and raped in order to maintain family honor and to be allowed to marry each other when otherwise their parents would not have permitted them to marry due to it not being seen as a good match. With Dinah and Shechem, it is an actual kidnapping and rape, and she is described as a young girl who is twelve years old (although if you actually plot it out by the years mentioned, she is nine).

Shechem then goes to Jacob and says he wants to marry Dinah. In Jubilees, Jacob and his sons are angry about what has happened, but in the Genesis version, we don't hear about what Jacob feels. Jacob is a cipher until the end. We also don't hear about what Dinah's brothers Simeon and Levi do—how they trick Shechem and his family. We're only told that they do trick them; in Genesis, this is spelled out. But since trickery is a major part of Israelite legends told in Genesis, it's not weird that trickery is part of the Genesis version of Dinah, which is dulled a bit in the Jubilees version. Dinah's brothers go to Shechem's town, rescue Dinah, and kill not only Shechem but all the men in the entire place. And they kill them in an especially brutal way, torturing them in some undescribed manner. Considering the cause of their attack, I think it's easy to conclude that they cut off their genitals. They then steal a bunch of things.

This chapter of Jubilees then goes on and on about how Israelites should not ever marry Gentiles. It comes up with dire punishments for Israelites who do that, whether they are men or women. We don't know if any such punishments were ever truly carried out. Neither Jubilees nor Genesis are history books, after all. It is about a particular truth, not a bunch of facts. But the Enochic and Biblical idea that separate categories should not be mixed is very strong in this story in Jubilees.

Gentiles certainly don't get off easy in this story either. They are massacred by Dinah's brothers. Subsequently, the entire local population is terrified of Jacob and his family. Jacob surprisingly scolds the brothers for what they have done, saying that now Jacob is going to have to be concerned about his own family being attacked in revenge. In Jubilees, Jacob has the last word. The Dinah story in Genesis ends differently, with the brothers responding to Jacob's scolding with, "Should our sister be treated like a whore?"

In neither version of the story does Dinah herself have a voice. I believe this is because she is a child, since Tamar, who is an adult and the victim of the other rape that is depicted in the Hebrew Bible, does have a voice. The Jubilees version of the Dinah story ends with praise especially for Levi, because he will be the ancestor of all the priests of the Temple. We are told repeatedly that he did the right thing.

Although it does not seem like it at first glance, the story of Dinah has a lot in common with the story of the Watchers. Sex between two different groups—in this case, Gentiles and Israelites instead of angels and humans—results in violence and destruction. One of the differences is that the violence is there at the beginning of the Jubilees story, with the kidnapping and rape, and there is emphasis on the innocence of the female who becomes the target of the Other. We never hear about the innocence of the wives in the Watchers story. Worse, later the wives are actually blamed, and the plot modified in some translations so that the wives not only "asked for it" but actually seduced the Watchers.

One lesson we can take from Jubilee's version of the Dinah story is that it's not just priests of the Temple who are problematic in terms of ritual impurity due to sexual transgressions but all of Israel and all Gentiles as well. The story puts the wrongness of the transgression in the foreground by having Dinah be a child and a person who is violently kidnapped and raped. This is different from the Watchers and women.

But something I have always wondered about the Watchers is whether the women in Enoch welcomed the sexual advances of the Watchers, whether they had any opportunity or power to refuse. Were they just objects to the Watchers who saw them as nothing more? In other (later) depictions of angels, they often sneer at humans and even say humans are impure and smell bad. This doesn't lead us to believe that the Watchers would be wooing these women. Also, I think most people who have ever worked with angels magically would not conceive of them in the form of dainty Victorian depictions of mild-eyed, androgynous pale and wispy people. Instead, many people I've known who have worked with angels in magic have described them as somewhat frightening and exuding power. If a supernatural being is frightening in aspect and wants to have sex with you, do you feel free to refuse? I think not. And if you assent, what's in it for you? Not much, since as a result you give birth to monsters, six at a time, "like lizards."

I think the Dinah-Shechem story is probably more like it would have been. The violence was there from the beginning and was not just something the Nephilim brought about. It was in the Watchers from day one and was passed on to their children like bad genes. Of course, this conclusion would imply that yes, evil not only came from Heaven but was somehow in it from the beginning. In my opinion, this fits with the very concept of the *bnei Elohim* as more like elevated spirits than mere angels.

The other parallel between the story of Dinah and the story of the Watchers is the similarity between Jacob and God. Many have commented on the fact that Jacob does not speak for most of the story. He only speaks at the end, when he scolds Simeon and Levi for killing all the men of Shechem. But who else was silent or didn't act, just as Jacob didn't act but let his sons do the acting? God was silent in part of the story of the Watchers. God didn't act until the archangels, in a similar position with respect to God as Jacob's sons were to him, came and spoke to God and remarked about the wailing of the souls of the dead and basically asked why God hadn't done anything. God does act then—to destroy the world, just as Simeon and Levi destroyed the world of Shechem. I think there is some deep truth beneath both these stories that links them in various ways—quietly but surely.

One thing both Enoch and Jubilees are firm about—only human beings can repent for their sins and be forgiven. Angels can repent all they want, but they won't be forgiven. I suspect that Jubilees' position would be the same with respect to Gentile repentance.

CHAPTER NINETEEN

The Book of Giants

There are two documents that are known as The Book of Giants. One of them has come to us through fragments in Aramaic and even Hebrew, which would make it older, and several fragmentary copies were found at Qumran (although they were not written there or written by the Essenes). The second one is the Manichean Book of Giants, which was based on the Aramaic Giants, and doesn't concern us here.

The Book of Giants we are talking about, the first one, retells the section of Enoch 6–16, only it is done from the point of view of the Nephilim, the sons of the Watchers. Whoever it was who copied the parts of Enoch known as The Watchers, The Book of Dreams, and The Epistle of Enoch, also copied Giants; it's the same handwriting and the same kind of parchment. Giants looks like it was sewn to the end of the other Enochic books mentioned.

Although his theory was eventually rejected, the scholar Milik argued that The Watchers was part of what he called the Enochic Pentateuch and was meant as an alternative to the Five Books of Moses. He found on one scroll at Qumran, The Astronomical Book and on the other, The Watchers, The Epistle of Enoch, The Book of Dreams, and Giants. He thought that Giants was written in the fourth century CE (most research shows only that it was written before the 2nd century CE) and that Enoch was translated into Greek in the sixth century CE. Most scholars nowadays reject the idea that Enoch was intended to be an alternate to the Pentateuch.

Giants features a character named Gilgamesh, but this person is not the same Gilgamesh as in the famous Babylonian epic. Nor does Giants look like a satire of the Babylonian Gilgamesh. Gilgamesh of Giants stands on his own. There's no evidence that the Israelites of the area where Enoch was found knew the Gilgamesh epic, but that doesn't mean the writer had never heard of it. There are similarities but they are of the same level as a college student might write about *The Brothers Karamazov* if they read the back cover of the paperback before a quiz. Some believe that the writer of Giants simply heard a conversation about the epic Gilgamesh and decided to riff off it, playing on the anti-Babylonian sentiment that was common at the time. It could certainly be seen as an anti-Pagan and anti-Gilgamesh epic.

Another scholar believes that Giants is a criticism of the Jewish Hellenists of the Upper Galilee and their religious practices. In that case, it has nothing to do with Babylon at all. Still other theories are that it was just meant to be anti-Pagan or anti-Gentile and didn't bother too much with any adherence to the Babylonian epic.

Giants and Gilgamesh have some names in common. Their protagonists are divine-human hybrids (in the epic Gilgamesh, being a divine-human hybrid is not a transgression), they both tell of wicked spirits, giant warriors, and mention Mount Hermon. Giants features a character named Hobabish, whose name is derived from Humbaba, the monster that Gilgamesh and Enkidu kill in the epic Gilgamesh. Both books are set in the time before the Flood. Outside of the epic story, Gilgamesh was depicted as a judge and ruler of the Underworld whom people would petition for help from pestering evil spirits. In Giants, Gilgamesh is one of the Nephilim who becomes a spirit—so in that world people would have needed to have him be exorcised rather than have him do any exorcising himself.

Dreams are important in both works. In the epic poem, Gilgamesh has some frightening dreams about the battle he will have with Humbaba. He goes to his mother for help in interpreting them. However, Giants doesn't even mention important figures of the epic Gilgamesh, like Enkidu or Ishtar.

Another big difference is that the epic Gilgamesh never suffers a major defeat, whereas in the Giants, he loses his war against humans and angels. Still, Giants doesn't make a big deal of that, and if it were meant to be a major critique of the epic Gilgamesh, it would have been depicted instead of just mentioned. Probably most important is that epic Gilgamesh is a hero, a good guy, and Giants Gilgamesh is not.

Although Giants does retell the story of the Watchers, here the angels are sent to Earth by God to teach humans how to be ethical, righteous, and ritually pure, but instead, they are seduced by women, have sex with them, and they father the Nephilim. Both Watchers and Nephilim do bad things and leak holy mysteries and secrets to women and men in Giants.

When Enoch heard about this, he asked God to help, and God gave some of the Giants dreams of warning. God also told Enoch to tell the Giants that if they repented, they would not be destroyed. The Giants sent one of their own to find Enoch and ask him to interpret their dreams. Enoch not only interpreted them but gave them two tablets with the explanation on it.

However, instead of repenting, many of the Giants just got worse. The fragments don't extend beyond that.

The Book of Giants

CHAPTER TWENTY

Other Books
of Enoch

There are two other books often related to Enoch: 2 Enoch and 3 Enoch.

2 Enoch

Also called The Slavonic Book of Enoch, since the oldest copy of it is written in Slavonic, most scholars believe 2 Enoch was translated into Greek from Aramaic by Hellenized Jews (some Hebrew words are simply transliterated rather than translated in it) and then into Slavonic by Christians. One scholar believes that learned people of the Hasidei Ashkenaz perhaps read 2 Enoch in Slavonic, which might have been brought to Germany by Jews who traveled in Eastern Europe, but this is hypothetical: there's no evidence of it historically.

There is no certainty about when this book was written. Guesses go from the 1st century CE to the 10th century CE—perhaps with the "core" originating in the 1st century CE. There are two versions available, a long one and a short one. Most scholars believe the longer version is more recent; it shows a very Christian influence, including the story of the Fallen Angels led by one called Satanail.

In this book we see the name of the children of the Watchers and their wives as "Grigori," which in turn is often translated into "Giants." This is based on the Greek translation of the word Nephilim.

The story of the Watchers' descent to Earth is included in 2 Enoch, but nothing is said about their teachings. Enoch begins as a man intimidated by the Watchers and develops into someone who becomes an angel himself and can speak directly to God. He travels through seven heavens in one version and ten heavens in the other. It's thought that the version with ten heavens is later.

One of the oddities of this version of Enoch's travels in Heaven is that he finds a hellish place in the third level of Heaven. This level contains a beautiful, peaceful place where the Tree of Life is located and where God rests when visiting that level. The angels tell Enoch that this is where righteous people will go at the end of time. But in the northern region of this third Heaven is a terrifying place of darkness where all sorts of torture occurs. This is the eternal inheritance of the wicked. Yet even this is not the final reward of the fallen angels (second heaven) and the Watchers (fifth heaven).

In the seventh heaven, as is portrayed or hinted at in other ascension texts, Enoch can see God from a distance, sitting on a high throne.

3 Enoch

The one "Book of Enoch" that has the strongest connection to magic is Sefer Hekhalot (The Book of Palaces), known in English as the The Hebrew Book of Enoch and usually cited as The Third Book of Enoch or 3 Enoch. The scholar Gershom Scholem thought this particular book was part of Hekhalot, and I think he was correct. It was the translator who renamed Sefer Hekhalot to The Hebrew Book of Enoch in 1928, primarily to take advantage of the mysteriousness and popularity of 1 Enoch, although it's certainly true that Enoch is a feature in this book. However, Enoch is presented to us in the form of the angel Metatron. This was the first work of Hekhalot that was translated into English. The earliest copies of it that have been found are from the 5th century CE, although one scholar argues that it's from the 9th to 10th century CE.

Although this book claims to have been written by Rav Ishmael, who is said to have been a priest in the Temple of Jerusalem, the real Rav Ishmael was not around until after the Romans destroyed the Temple, so it could not have been him who wrote this. But we should not be surprised, since many ancient books are pseudepigraphic. What is more interesting is that this is a book about a man's ascent to Heaven, where he meets Metatron and sees the face of God. Metatron tells him that when he was Enoch, he was raised up to Heaven together with the Shekhinah, who previously had lived on Earth but who was removed from it due to the rampant idolatry being practiced by humans.

An interesting connection with 1 Enoch is that various angels bow to Metatron, and a number of them rule over precisely the forbidden knowledge that the Watchers shared with human beings: fire, hail, wind, lightning, thunder, snow, rain, day, night, sun, moon, planets, and constellations. Metatron himself is transformed into various aspects of fire, in keeping with the Hebrew angels being Fire spirits. We are told that Metatron is the Prince of the Presence (which recalls the figure in Jubilees and also one of the archangels from The Book of Enoch, Phanuel, whose name can roughly be translated to Face of God).

Various angel names and what they rule over are featured in 3 Enoch. We also get a complete description of the Throne, which has aspects of storm as well as fire, and all the names of the angels that control each part of this complex object. Metatron shows Rav Ishmael all the letters written on the Throne that control the various parts of creation—everything from plants to the stars to the Throne itself. He is shown various unmixable things, like hail and fire, that combine without obliterating each other through the use of the names of God. He is also shown the spirits of the righteous dead and the yet unborn, the destroying angels of Sheol with their names, and much more. We learn a number of Divine Names as well as the seventy names of Metatron. There is much to conjure with in this book. However, one of the big differences that I noticed between this book and those considered characteristic of Hekhalot is that we do not get any of the use of names or "seals" that allow the ascender to pass through all seven heavens safely. However, Peter Schafer, a well-known scholar of Hekhalot, says that the ascension is not the central part of Hekhalot works,

Other Books of Enoch

171

as Scholem claimed; it's the adjuration of angels that is central. In other words, Hekhalot is about magic, not spirituality or mysticism. There is plenty of material for adjuration in 3 Enoch, although it does not specifically say that's what it's for.

Some scholars consider that Enochic writings contributed to the formation of the Hekhalot practice, and especially as it is described in 3 Enoch; other scholars think they have nothing to do with each other. It's true that centuries come between the two groups of texts and nowhere is there any mention of a connection between them. Nor do we have any evidence of secret groups that preserved 1 Enoch and involved themselves in 3 Enoch.

The practice of Hekhalot has a known connection to Babylonian magic, and 3 Enoch 4:5–6 is where the strongest emphasis on magic is in this book. This section might well have been handed down from one magic worker to another.

Daniel Davila, a prominent scholar of Merkavah and Hekhalot, says that there are similarities between 3 Enoch and Similitudes from 1 Enoch. Reed argues that the section about Metatron in 3 Enoch might have been inspired by The Watchers that Christians preserved. I don't feel that there's much evidence for the figure of Metatron to have been influenced by The Watchers, because not only is the name Metatron not even mentioned in 1 Enoch, but it isn't mentioned as the angel who sits on a throne before God until the 5th century CE, by which time 1 Enoch had been rejected by both Christians and Jews; few would be familiar with the story of the Watchers by that time.

This book was used by the Hasidei Ashkenaz, who were known practitioners of magic, including golem-making, and some sources for it might have been preserved by Christians. The Watchers, written by Jews, was allowed to disappear during the Rabbinic period but was preserved by Christians (at least, for a while longer), and Jews might in turn have borrowed it back.

Late in terms of Hekhalot, I don't find the thoery that 3 Enoch was a predecessor to Hekhalot as a whole believable. On the other hand, we're told that early works of Hekhalot depict someone ascending to Heaven with a guide, and later works of Hekhalot show how to do it yourself. There are also ideas newer than Merkavah literature in 3 Enoch, which is a bit older than Hekhalot.

CHAPTER TWENTY-ONE

Enoch in Occulture

Asael is mentioned in all sorts of items involved in Jewish magic. He's identified in spell books from the Cairo Genizah. His name is inscribed on Babylonian incantation bowls, written on amulets from the Land of Israel, and found in Greco-Egyptian magical texts like *The Greek Magical Papyri* (PGM). In those works, he is not demonic or evil. On the contrary, he is an angel that magic workers can appeal to for help. To me this says that he can be adjured in angel magic without the issue of raising a demon by accident. And for those who do work with demons, Asael is not a problem.

Enoch himself is asked for help on some of the Babylonian incantation bowls. A few bowls mention Mount Hermon, which is where the Watchers made their oath to have sex with women.

Witchblood and the Nephilim

Some believe in "witchblood"—an inherited, genetic feature peculiar to actual witches. Many of those who hold this idea don't believe that those who have not been born with witchblood can ever be witches.

Some say this belief is modeled on the Enochic story of the Watchers coming down to Earth, having sex with women, and producing the Nephilim, which people often style as "Giants." But in my opinion, in no way could the Nephilim ever be the ancestors of witches, because for one thing, the Nephilim were completely unmagical. Remember, they raped and killed all human beings, they sexually assaulted and killed all the animals, including birds and fish, they killed and ate each other, and they despoiled the Earth. This does not sound like any sort of witchcraft to me. Not to mention that the Nephilim didn't have any children, which kind of negates any possibility that they were the ultimate source of witchblood.

The Watchers are another story. They brought forbidden knowledge to human beings, which included not only astrology but root-cutting, binding and reversing spells, and various methods of divination. These skills, not the brutality of the Nephilim, are treasures for magic workers. But remember with whom those skills were shared: people. If witches are to look back upon ancestors for inspiration, it should be not to the Nephilim or even the Watchers but to our human ancestors who received that knowledge and most likely maintained it. Also, for Enoch, magical knowledge is preserved in language, specifically, in writing. That makes a hash of the often-met objection that "real" magic is only passed on orally, especially when we recall how often a practice is interlaced with grimoire magic, for example, traditional (European) witchcraft, Vodou, and so forth. I think this kind of eclecticism is something to be proud of rather than to disdain. Being eclectic seems to be a fundamental human trait.

The story of angels coming to Earth and having children with women inspires modern practitioners of magic, especially when we consider the forbidden knowledge that the Watchers shared with humans. I understand that. But the Watchers story is not the only example of this in human culture.

In his introduction to *The Book of Enoch the Prophet*, magic practitioner Lon Milo DuQuette states that we don't know enough about Enoch to understand it. I think that this is true for most of us, and it throws into relief the flaw in modeling ourselves after figures in the story. He also points out that the The Book of Enoch that has come down to us doesn't have anything to do with Enochian magic, the Elizabethan astrologer and magician John Dee, his occultist/scryer friend Edward Kelley, the sorcerer Aleister Crowley, or any other prominent magician.

He does mention Madame Blavatsky's book *The Secret Doctrine,* wherein she is quite fanciful about Enoch and who the Watchers represent. Personally, I cannot give her interpretation of the Elohim as alien spacemen any credibility. For me, alien spacemen have no place in magic or religion. They are a materialist incursion into the spiritual and magical universe, which can exist just fine without spacemen. Your lightyears may vary.

The one thing that DuQuette brings up as a valid source for magicians in Enoch is the part where names of angels and their field of proficiency are listed. For the interested practitioner, I would combine those lists with searches in magical literature for mentions of those angels (or demons, for that matter) working with magicians after the ancient period. Some of them are there.

Dee searched for The Book of Enoch for many years, perhaps because Enoch had a reputation as an astrologer and Dee was an astrologer himself. DuQuette wonders if perhaps Dee did have access to Enoch due to the dispersion of the libraries of English abbeys from 1536–1539, but we don't find any note of it in his library catalogs or his own writings. He asked the angel Il about Enoch in 1583, and people often refer to his book about communing with angels as "Enoch."

Some have considered that Sloane MS. 3189 is the Enoch-related book that Dee refers to during his travels in 1586, but if you look at it, you can see it has nothing to do with The Book of Enoch or Enoch the Biblical figure. It is composed of tables of numbers in Enochian (angelic) letters scried by Edward Kelley during contact with the angels combined with Dee's notes on his conversations with angels. The Enochian letters have nothing to do with The Book of Enoch; they are not Hebrew or Aramaic letters. You can see this and many other manuscripts at the British Library's website, where they give access to a large and digitized collection of various things that help a person fiddle away hours of enjoyment.

"Enochic" refers to ancient Jewish literature and perhaps groups that are connected in some way to The Book of Enoch. "Enochian" is a magical

Enoch in Occulture

language that has nothing to do with ancient Enochic texts. It is an angelic language according to two Elizabethan occultists: John Dee and Edward Kelley.

Dee never referred to the angelic language as "Enochian." The angels told him it was called "Logaeth." Likewise, there is no evidence that Enochian has any relationship to Ethiopic. For me, the strongest connection between The Book of Enoch and Enochian is that both involved speaking with angels. But then so do various magic books about calling down angels for magical purposes, as well as many other magical practices of various cultures.

One scholar's explanation for Dee's strong interest in finding Enoch ties it to the fear of a coming apocalypse and need to recover secret or lost knowledge to deal with such an event. This strikes me as pertinent to our own period—the scent of doom in the air has people scrambling for keys to understand and perhaps influence what is or will be occurring. I think this goes a long way toward explaining the intense interest in Enoch today.

In short, Enochian and Enochic have no connection in fact.

Conclusion

There is so much we can learn from Enoch. One of my favorite aspects of this book is how it preserves various versions of the Watchers' story, in this way allowing for multiple voices and perspectives to live together in the text, to resonate with and tumble over each other. It reminds me of Cubist art, which tried to depict objects from multiple perspectives at the same time. This is certainly not something we expect from an ancient sacred text; we expect such texts to be monologic, to have one single, unified, authoritative (and some would claim, authoritarian) voice. It is surprising and refreshing when such texts are not. Yes, the bad guys do get nailed to the wall—except 10 percent of them get to live on. Nothing is absolute, not even the Divine, who is not always paying attention or listening.

What do we learn from Enoch? What is the forbidden knowledge, and what is hidden? There is a rich assortment of bodies of knowledge in Enoch. We hear of various sorts of magic, like those that involve the use of Divine Names. We're told that those names are used wrongly by Shemihazah to make curses, oaths, and spells, but historically the use of Divine Names for magical purposes (including spells and even death curses) has not been forbidden in Judaism (see my book, *The Magic of the Sword of Moses*). The pronunciation of Divine Names to achieve the gift of prophecy has been advocated by medieval rabbis such as Abraham Abulafia, who taught the technique to others; it is still practiced today.

We hear of root-cutting, a magical practice with plants that was practiced by Babylonian exorcists but also by country folk in 19-century England and shamanic healers today. In fact, today, working with plants magically is even more prevalent than it was in the past, and having done it myself, I have certainly not found anything harmful in the work, only in terms of people assuming they have a magical or spiritual knowledge of plants that they actually lack, which means they might do harm to themselves or others by accident, out of ignorance.

Astrology does come in for a bit of a bashing in Enoch, but some of the most respected magic workers I have known have been astrologers, who used their knowledge of the stars not only for divination but for activities like protection. I have not known any to be possessed by or under the sway of demons. On the contrary, many work directly with the angels that inhabit, for instance, the Fixed Stars (stars that appear not to move from how we see them on Earth).

From Enoch, we also learn the names of a variety of angels and the bodies of knowledge over which they have special control. We can choose to ignore the fact that each angel is identified for us by name, but why would we be given their names if not to call upon them for help (knowing the names of demons was not considered necessary for Jewish exorcists)? It is as if embedded in the text is the knowledge that at least some of these angels will be rehabilitated and work with human beings in a positive way.

We are often told that Enoch is a cautionary tale about seeking knowledge that is hidden or secret, knowledge that we have no right to, and that we should stay in our lane (see Ben Sirah's remarks about knowing our place with respect to secrets). I do not believe that. For one, as a former teacher, I am certain that the problem is not esoteric knowledge. The problem is us. And that is a transient problem, because we can change. Change is a quintessential property of mortals. Change is within our power.

For instance, Shemihazah used Divine Names to do (apparently) dark magic. But there is nothing wrong with using Divine Names for magic.

We can see this in *The Sword of Moses* and other magic books in the long tradition of Jewish angel magic. The knowledge of the names is not the problem. We are. If anything, that's clear in Enoch. After all, nothing is wrong with metalworking, which is a body of secret knowledge. The problem is using it to kill people instead of as tools to grow plants.

We also see this in terms of the figure of Enoch himself. Talk about change! This guy went from a completely nothing-special person, a scribe, not a priest, not a big-shot Patriarch, never worked any miracles, and he not only became immortal but morphed into the Prince of the Presence, who can gaze at the fiery face of God without being burned to a crisp and who sits and writes before the divine throne. Surely his story encourages us to change and to strive for greater spiritual achievement.

One of the stepping stones to knowledge in Enoch is language. Here (and elsewhere) Hebrew is a tool for the acquisition and wielding of knowledge and supernatural power gained through opening channels of communication with the other world. It is a means of making magic a la Shemihazah and his uses of the Divine Name but also in terms of learning hidden and forbidden things, such as secrets hidden in the Hebrew Bible itself. And historically, in Hekhalot, it was precisely the mastery of Hebrew that people asked as a boon from the angels they adjured, because to know Hebrew is to learn the hidden magical secrets of the Hebrew Bible that nestle beneath each word. We also see that Hebrew is an aid to the attainment of vision, as Enoch shows us.

I firmly believe that Hebrew is indeed a powerful magical tool, but I would say that other languages can function similarly, especially if they are not one's native language. Learning another language changes a person. We are forced to see through completely different eyes and then notice things that were not previously visible to us. I highly recommend language as a means of magic and mysticism.

Enoch was, yes, raised up to Heaven by the Divine. It was not something he did all on his own through his own hard work. But he first made himself into someone who would not only deserve that but who would

Conclusion

survive seeing the face of God. That was from his own work, not from a gift from the angels or God. He did that through study, staying on the divine course, and being willing to help others, even the Nephilim.

One of the problems I have seen with people attempting to elevate themselves in a mystical or magical way is the sense of entitlement, such that some people seem to almost expect to achieve incredibly difficult things quickly and easily, as if they are an exception as a human being. I think most of us know that we are not exceptions, which is fine. We don't need to be. You don't have to be a genius to be a good musician or artist, and you don't need witchblood to be a good magic worker. You need the same two things as any endeavor: theory and practice. Even mystics have to study their holy books and to practice prayer, meditation, and good works. The only sure thing is that there is no easy, quick way.

The difference between Enoch's learning and the wives' learning is partly the difference between the source of the knowledge—holy angels vs. not so holy angels, or angels who gave their knowledge freely and angels who gave knowledge in exchange for sexual favors or in some other transactional way, such that they received something as payment for that knowledge. I sometimes think this trading of knowledge for something else was precisely what "corrupted" the knowledge, if it was corrupted at all. Or we could look at it from the perspective that with Enoch, knowledge was given as a reward for his righteousness, whereas with the Watchers, knowledge was to some extent given as a reward for sex.

But that's not all there is to it. The types of forbidden knowledge at the center of Enoch are two-fold. Almost all of them can be used for good or ill, and that is up to us. The same thing that meant we no longer were appropriate for the playpen of Eden—eating the fruit of the Tree of Knowledge of Good and Evil—means that we can make choices about how to use any knowledge we gain. We can't be thrown out of the Garden again for it.

For me, knowledge, forbidden or not, is not anywhere near as problematic for us as is the Nephilim.

Because we *are* the Nephilim. And that is the most forbidden of all the knowledge that Enoch brings us.

Like them, we always want things to be bigger than necessary to match our own over-estimation of ourselves, our grotesque selfishness, our bloated self-image. Our meals and portions must be much larger than necessary to keep our body healthy, more than is even pleasurable. We assign the phrase "metabolically necessary" to our consumption of other animals—our appetites are so big that we must kill to satisfy them. Our need for larger and larger homes demands the despoiling of great tracts of the wild that were homes for other creatures who are pushed out into narrower and narrower strips of the land and sea and who are killed if they make the mistake of trying to live alongside us. We need bigger and bigger cars to feed our enormous fear of other humans and our gigantic vanity. We have poisoned the vastness of the air and in doing so, killed many of its creatures. Even when we run away from the cities we see as poisonous, we demand massive quantities of land to surround our new country retreat—and we light it up like an airport because our fear of the dark and of our own neighbors is so huge. We are enormously reckless with ourselves, poisoning our water with bits of plastic so tiny that they can now be found lodged in our hearts, where they can release their toxins secretly and incrementally, the tiny things that will take down the big things—what's more, tiny things that we ourselves engendered. Our own body fat and our mothers' milk are full of molecular level poisons like endocrine disruptors that we've used to scent our shampoo and cleaning products. Our waste of what we have and throw away hardly used forms vast islands in our oceans. We wonder why so many of us get cancer when every day everything we own is bleeding toxins, from the dyes in our clothes to the pesticides in our foods and the fragrances in our homes. The seasons are out of order and more and more, just as Enoch foretold, we can't rely on our climate due to our own activities.

And like the Nephilim, we love killing. We glorify it in our culture and spend billions of dollars and lives on our endless wars and on the guns we need to sate our huge fears and gigantic, poisonous hates. We not only see ourselves as Giants, but our country as the biggest giant that has the right and even the duty to overwhelm the rest of the world and leave nowhere that has not known the dark of our enormous, grim shadow.

No archangels are nagging the Divine to act, but the Earth acts, a bigger Giant than we could ever dream of being. It repays our Nephilimic behavior with droughts, fires, floods, massive windstorms, killing heat and dire cold, lightning that causes huge forest fires whose smoke chokes us and that even come to destroy our homes like avenging fire spirits/angels. And more.

The difference between how the Nephilim destroyed and how the Earth destroys is that the Earth is doing it to survive and preserve most life, whereas the Nephilim did it basically for sport. I am not sure if the Nephilim had to do evil because of who they were, if it was for the hell of it, but I know for us it is not built in. We can choose to live differently and to help heal the Earth and ourselves. And we can do it with the help of the spirits, of the Divine, if we are open to it.

The Watchers have a number of things to teach us. One of the biggest is that there is no expanse of space between the heavens and the earth. And I mean that not merely in the sense of ground and sky, but in the larger sense of the connection between spirits and people. The channels of communication are there for us to learn to use not just to speak but to listen. We do not need to use particular prayers. We can study sacred texts, whether they be in print or written in the pattern of a cat's stripes or the creases of petals, the scent of summer or the feel of the sun on a cool day, the taste of ripe fruit or bitter leaves. It is possible for spirits to live among us and to share their knowledge with us. This says a lot positive about working with angels in various old-school ways. That is one of the oldest types of magic that we know of, and the foundation of Jewish magic. But spirits are also a presence in all sorts of religions and mysticism, which are, yes, ways of knowing.

Another thing we can learn from the Watchers is that it's possible to screw up and yet be redeemed for it. We see that in how we are told in

Enoch that the bad Watchers were walled up in lightless holes filled with sharp rocks as punishment for what they did, but we also see their names used in positive magic centuries later. How did that happen? Something occurred that freed them from darkness and selfishness and allowed them to morph into beings who are gracious helpers and teachers. We know that they were sorry for what they did—they asked for divine forgiveness and to be allowed back into Heaven—but we also know that they experienced grief—the great grief of seeing their own beloved children killed in the Flood. Grief changes a person, and I would wager it could even change an angel, especially one who had lived so long among humans. Those who have lost a loved one know this truth deeply. Grief can make a person bitter or debilitated, but it can also result in a resolution that we do what needs to be done *now*. For now is all we, as mortals, actually have.

It might well be that those angels who fooled around and found out learned from the bitter fruit of grief and changed. Some believe that The Book of Enoch teaches that angels can't repent; only humans can do that. But I think the proof of repentance—which is not just feeling bad for the past but living in such a way as to mend it—is in the continued appearance of some of the angels in the history of magic and mysticism.

I also feel that this resonates with our own situation as modern-day Nephilim. The Nephilim of ancient days didn't have the opportunity— or maybe even the capability—of regretting what they'd done, changing their behavior, and making amends. But the Watchers tried to change, and some of them apparently even did. We can do the same. We do not have to continue to be stuck inside of our Nephilim skins, trapped by our own cruelty and ruthlessness, strangling inside our deadly bigness.

Nor do we have to trudge around feeling ashamed of what humans have done. These words are not a call for us to castigate ourselves and hang our heads. Not at all. I have never seen scolding act as a positive force. On the contrary, I see the recognition of wrongdoing as positive, opening the portal to growth. We cannot move on if we do not first accept where we are.

God sees the truth and does nothing. That's because we are not in the time before. We are in the now, the human, mortal time. We are out of the

Conclusion

playpen of the Garden and in the midst of the historical world. The job of mending the world is not God's.

It's ours.

I hope The Book of Enoch inspires you as it has inspired me to work on that.

APPENDIX

Timeline of
The Book of Enoch

300 BCE	The Astronomical Book written in Aramaic in Judea
300 BCE	The Book of the Watchers written in Aramaic in Judea. Probably written by scribes associated with the Temple of Jerusalem.
Around the time of the Maccabean Revolt (167–160 BCE)	The Book of Dreams
Around the time of the Maccabean Revolt (167–160 BC)	Epistle of Enoch
2nd century BCE	The Book of Enoch put together, except the Similitudes. Instead, The Book of Giants was often included.
1st century CE	The Similitudes or The Book of Parables written, probably by a Jewish Christian. It replaces The Book of Giants in The Book of Enoch.
2nd century CE	Jews begin rejecting The Book of Enoch because the Rabbis didn't accept the idea that angels could sin.

3rd and 4th century CE	Christians begin rejecting The Book of Enoch.
350–500 CE	Translated from Greek to Ethiopic and becomes part of the canon of Ethiopic Orthodox Tewahedo Church.
1773	James Bruce, a Scottish traveler, brings back three copies of The Book of Enoch in Ge'ez.
1821	Richard Laurence, an English scholar of ancient Hebrew, translates The Book of Enoch from Ge'ez.
1906	RH Charles, Irish Anglican theologian, translates The Book of Enoch from Ge'ez.
1951–1976	Aramaic fragments of Enoch found at Qumran.
1976	Milik translates the Aramaic fragments into English.

Glossary

ben adam: A human being, also a righteous person.

bnei Elohim: "sons" (but also just means children) of the Elohim, which can mean God, gods, holy spirits like angels, or human bigwigs like kings.

Cherubim: Fire spirits who usually are literally connected with the throne of God. Their single calf-like leg holds the wheel within a wheel that allows the Chariot to move without the Cherubim turning their four faces.

Elohim: A word that can mean God, gods, holy spirits like angels, or humans like kings. Can also be plural for God, which raises questions about the state of things in the very early parts of Genesis.

Enoch: An ancient scribe who is described in Genesis as being "taken" by God at his end rather than dying. He is an important figure in The Book of Enoch, learning forbidden knowledge from the angels in Heaven. Enoch is an intermediary between the Watchers and the Nephilim on Earth and YHVH in Heaven.

Enochic: A word for things associated with The Book of Enoch in terms of its figures and/or ideology.

Enochian: A term invented by the Elizabethan scryer Edward Kelley as the name for a language the angels he was in contact with used.

Halakhah: The Ten Commandments plus all the ways they were unfolded in the Hebrew Bible and the Talmud, to add up to 613 Commandments.

Kadosh: Meaning "holy." Part of the hymn the angels sing to YHVH, *Kadosh, kadosh, kadosh* (Holy, holy, holy), which is also included in the Jewish liturgy so that we might sing with them.

Kashrut: A system for ensuring ritual purity is maintained in the choice, storage, and preparation of food.

Metatron: An archangel that many consider was the final form of Enoch in Heaven. He is not mentioned in The Book of Enoch.

Mishnah: The first major work of Rabbinic Judaism, composed during the first three centuries of the first millennium.

Nephilim: The rapacious giants born of the union between the Watchers and their human wives.

root-cutting: A magical practice that was practiced by Babylonian exorcists, ancient Greeks, and European country folk in 19th-century England and by shamanic healers today. It involves harvesting herbs at particular times of year or day, under particular stars, or particular moon phases in order for the plant to work best for magical and/or medical uses.

Shekhinah: The feminine aspect of YHVH, who lived on Earth until it became overrun with sin due to the actions of the Watchers, the Nephilim, and people. She was then raised up to Heaven along with Enoch. Periodically she is experienced by people on Earth during especially peaceful or sanctified moments. She is more well known in the Kabbalah than in ancient writings.

YHVH: The first name of God. Hebrew is often written without vowels, and because only the High Priest of the Temple of Jerusalem was supposed to pronounce the name YHVH at certain times of the year, it was traditionally written without vowels. However, the vowels of the Hebrew name for "Lord" were written as part of the name in liturgical texts so that readers would know to say *Adonai*. Christians interpreted these as the vowels of YHVH and morphed that name into Jehovah. Most people pronounce this name by reading the consonant names, like YodHayVavHay, or refer to it as *Ha Shem* ("The Name"), or as the Tetragrammaton.

Notes

1. The Sadducees were an elite group focused on the hereditary priesthood during the time of the Second Temple. They maintained the Temple of Jerusalem and were important in Judean politics and society. They were Hellenized and rejected the oral Torah, the idea of spirits, and the resurrection of the dead. They ran the Temple and conducted the sacrificial cult.
2. The Zadokite priesthood was a strict Jewish sect that broke from mainstream Judaism and settled in Damascus, Syria, in the second century BCE. The Zadokites claimed to descend from Zadok, the priest appointed by Samuel.
3. Hekhalot (Palaces) was a Jewish mystical practice that overlaps with the writings of Merkavah but generally came later, from late antiquity to the early Middle Ages. Hekhalot texts contain magical operations; Merkavah does not.
4. Merkavah (also transliterated as Merkabah) is a type of Jewish mysticism. It centered on practices to achieve the vision of the throne of God (the "Chariot"), which is first described in Ezekiel. Its texts, such as Ma'aseh Merkavah, were written between 200-700 CE, although some were written far later, in Germany in the Middle Ages.
5. -im can also be found as a feminine dual ending for words like *yadim* (hands), which makes me wonder if what is being indicated by this name is a combo masculine/feminine god.
6. Over and over the impossible combination of fire and ice is seen in descriptions of Heaven in Judaism. I believe this combination of ultimately unmixable things is important with respect to the prohibition of mixing categories that should stay separate in Enoch.
7. Blue is the quintessential color of Heaven (for obvious reasons) in many religions.

8. Songs of the Sabbath Sacrifice contains hymns for each of the first thirteen sabbaths of the Hebrew year. It was probably written around 100 BCE, and even though multiple copies were found at Qumran, the sect located there didn't write it. For one thing, they used "Elohim" as the name of God, which the Qumran folks didn't use. The text describes the divine throne room, what the angels there were like, and how the angels around the throne of the Divine worshipped. This text uses imagery from Ezekiel, Isaiah, Exodus, and, most pertinent for us, Enoch.

9. A bit of wonkiness occurs here, since Ezekiel existed after Enoch in the timeline of documents, but Enoch occurs before the Flood and so, of course, before Ezekiel saw his vision.

10. Hellenization was the adoption of Greek language, culture, and religion in the lands that were conquered by Alexander and others. The two main centers of Hellenized Judaism were in Alexandria in Egypt and Antioch in Syria, but the Temple of Jerusalem also came under the influence of Hellenism during the Second Temple Period. Later, with the rise of Jewish nationalism and the oppression of Judaism under Antiochus IV, Hellenism lost favor.

11. The Second Temple stood between 516 BCE and 70 CE, when it was destroyed by the Romans. Please note that although this temple was destroyed, there were others that provided the people access to the sacrificial cult at the time, especially in the northern part of the Land of Israel. The Second Temple replaced the Temple of Solomon, which was destroyed by the Babylonians. Jews who returned from their exile in Babylon, many of whom were from the temple priesthood, were involved in building the Second Temple to replace Solomon's Temple. Herod the Great, about whom many false stories have been spun (the slaughter of the innocents never happened, for example), refurbished the Second Temple, and so people at the time often called it Herod's Temple. This was the largest sacred temple in the ancient world, and if you notice what Al-Aqsa is built on top of, you will see its Western Wall below the foundation. So yes, the Second Temple was there almost 1,000 years before the mosque, and the Temple of Solomon was even older.

12. Antiochus IV ruled the Seleucid Empire from 175–164 BCE. He persecuted the Jews of Judea and Samaria, apparently because he thought they were planning a rebellion. Antiochus decided that he should be the one to select the High Priest at the Temple of Jerusalem, but while the king was out making war against the Romans, the priests at the Temple kicked out Antiochus' choice and put their own choice in. Antiochus assaulted Jerusalem and put his man

Menelaus back in as High Priest, plus executed thousands of Jewish civilians and sold thousands into slavery. He went on to desecrate the Temple.

13. Rabbinism (also written as "Rabbinics") emerged following the destruction of the Jerusalem Temple as an attempt to reorganize Judaism around sacred writings, rather than the sacrificial cult, which was no longer available. It substituted prayer, Halakhah, and study of sacred texts for the sacrificial cult and eventually became the basis of Judaism. The important figures of Rabbinisn are referred to as "the Rabbis."

14. The Hasidei Ashkenaz (German Pietists) were a group of Jewish mystics who mostly lived in the Rhineland of Germany in the 12th–13th centuries. They were extremely strict in their observance and looked upon other, less observant, Jews with disdain. They created a "Law of Heaven" that was above the regular Halakhah. One of their number was Eleazar of Worms, who is cited as the author of directions for creating a golem and who is alleged to have written the magic book, The Book of Abramelin.

15. Gnosticism is typified by a belief in a dual Divine (perhaps one apparent god, which is evil, and one hidden god, which is good), that the material world is evil, that the divine spark exists in all people, and, in the Christian form, that Jesus was not material but a kind of ghost who only appeared to suffer. The first academic scholar of Kabbalah, Gershom Scholem, believed that the Kabbalah had gnostic influences, but later scholars, such as Moshe Idel, proved this wrong.

16. Syncellus was the name of a church office. George Syncellus lived during the 8th century CE. He wrote Extract of Chronicles, which was composed of many tables of historical events in chronological order but also includes extensive quotes from other texts, including Enoch.

17. The Aksumite Kingdom existed from classical antiquity (around 150 BCE) to the Middle Ages in the area of what is now known as Ethiopia and Eritrea, and at one point extended into southern Arabia. Greek was the common language, but Ge'ez was the court language. Christianity became the state religion in the 4th century CE. After the Muslim invasion of the 7th century CE, which cut off the kingdom from the Christian centers of Byzantium and Rome, Ge'ez replaced Greek in the area. The kingdom began to decline in isolation and collapsed in 960 CE.

18. Charles (1855–1921) was a professor of theology from Northern Ireland. He translated many apocryphal books, including The Book of Enoch in 1906.

19. The Epic of Gilgamesh was written in Mesopotamia in the 18th century BCE and tells the story of the hero Gilgamesh. It was put together from various older Sumerian stories.

Notes   **193**

20. Some scholars believe that the astronomical theories in The Astronomical Book are borrowed from Babylon, but many others argue that these theories are original to ancient Israel. Still others say it's not clear where these theories came from. I think it's important to keep in mind that, in the past, it was a common approach to scholarship of ancient Hebrew texts to always look for sources outside of the Land of Israel, as if the Israelites couldn't come up with anything of their own. This is no longer an acceptable approach to ancient Hebrew texts.

21. These are stories of the seventh king in a royal line who had to do with the flood in Babylonian mythology.

22. Although "Giborim" is often presented as a class of being, perhaps "great men of ancient times," it's really a description and can be applied to, for instance, lions.

23. The Testaments of the Twelve Patriarchs is a pseudepigraphic apocalyptic work said to be written by the twelve sons of Jacob. It was written originally in Hebrew or Greek and took its final form in the 2nd century CE. Scholars still don't know whether this was based on a Jewish work that was modified by Christians or if it was originally a Christian work. It is composed of ethical advice.

24. Chapters 3–14 of 2 Esdras is known as 4 Ezra, a Jewish apocalyptic work that was incorporated into 2 Esdras. It was written in Hebrew in the first century CE after the destruction of the Temple of Jerusalem and then translated into Greek, Latin, Armenian, Ethiopian, and Georgian. It's part of the canon of the Ethiopian Orthodox Church. It describes seven visions of Ezra the scribe.

25. The Essenes probably split from the Zadokite priests and considered the priesthood that had been appointed at the time of the Maccabee Revolt to be illegitimate. They thought of themselves as legitimate instead and were thoroughly on board with the hierarchy of the sacrificial cult. They were celibate, vegetarian, didn't believe in money or private property, and lived in communities where everything was shared. They apparently practiced magic because they placed a high value on knowing the names of the angels. They rejected violence except in self-defense and refused to own slaves. They bathed every morning as a means of ritual purification. They are usually thought to be identical to the people of Qumran, but they were located all over, including in Syria, and did not live in Qumran itself.

26. Just because it was not found there does not mean it wasn't written at that time. The Book of Esther wasn't found there either, but it existed then.

27. The Book of Giants was once known only in its Manichaean version, which was far afield in China, but more recently several fragments in Aramaic and in Hebrew were found at Qumran. Giants retells the Watchers' story but focuses

on the Nephilim (the Giants). Some scholars believe that its origins are older than Enoch.

28. The Temple Scroll, a pseudepigraph attributed to Moses, describes in detail the Temple as King Solomon should have built it instead of how he actually did. It was written in Hebrew during the Second Temple period. Some say it was written in Qumran and others that it was written by a rebellious group of Zadokites; no one knows for certain. Ritual purity is an important topic in this text, which might remind us of the people of Qumran and the Essenes.

29. The Hasmoneans were governmental administrators and Temple functionaries installed when the Holy Land was under the control of the Seleucid Empire, from 140 BCE to 37 BCE. The Seleucid Empire was ruled by descendants of Alexander the Great's generals. The Hasmoneans were much hated and highly Hellenized. The Hasmonean rulership was finally replaced by Herod the Great.

30. Josiah was the 16th king of Judah and lived from 640-609 BCE. He is most remembered for conducting major reforms of Judaic practice, including eliminating any official worship of gods other than YHVH, mostly meaning Baal but also referring the "the heavenly hosts," which were interpreted as angels or stars—now what does that remind you of? Josiah also destroyed many local places of Jewish worship, often referred to as High Places. He went so far as to destroy Pagan altars outside of his kingdom.

31. Ezra was a priest and scribe who returned from exile in Babylon and set about starting a reform that centered Judaism on Mosaic law instead of just on the sacrificial cult. As a functionary of the Persian King Ataxerxes II, Ezra had the power to back up demands that people start obeying Torah law: honoring the Sabbath, an annual tax to support the Temple, and quit marrying Gentiles. He got men to divorce their foreign wives.

32. The Genesis Apocryphon, written between the third century BCE to the first century CE in Hasmonean Aramaic, is a retelling of events described in Enoch, Jubilees, and Genesis, focusing especially on Lamech, Noah, and Abraham. It was one of the first documents found at Qumran in 1946.

33. Neopythagoreanism was a movement in Hellenism to bring back mysticism. It refocused on the soul and its wish to be united with the Divine. It arose in the first century BCE and continued until the first to the second century CE.

34. In traditional Judaism, texts that include Divine Names are not to be thrown out; instead, they are buried, usually after being wrapped in a prayer shawl. But what if you accrue 400,000 of them? Then you put them in a genizah, a storeroom for such texts. This is what happened to a huge mass of texts and

fragments in the Ben Ezra synagogue in Old Cairo, Egypt. This storeroom was walled up but was discovered by Europeans in the late 18th century.

35. In the Hebrew Bible, the books designated as "Prophets" include Joshua, Judges, Samuel, Kings, Isaiah, Jeremiah, Ezekiel, Hosea, Joel, Amos, Obadiah, Jonah, Micah, Nahum, Habakkuk, Zephaniah, Haggai, Zechariah, and Malachi.

36. Wisdom (also known as Writings) is composed of the following in the Hebrew Bible: Psalms, Proverbs, Job, Song of Songs, Ruth, Lamentations, Ecclesiastes, Esther, Daniel, Ezra and Nehemiah, and Chronicles

37. The Mishnah is the first major work of Rabbinic Judaism and is composed of teachings that were formerly passed down from the Pharisees' oral teachings. The language is partly Mishnaic Hebrew and partly Aramaic. It was composed in the first three centuries of the first millennium.

38. The Tosefta is composed of the oral teachings and was written mostly in Mishnaic Hebrew in 189 CE. It's a supplement of the Mishna.

39. Midrashic writing involves the analysis of texts by looking at the roots of words, at their numerical equivalents, at words that aren't included (what is left unsaid), and even at each letter.

40. Genesis Rabbah is a Midrashic text written between 300-500 CE that deals with Genesis, expanding on, interpreting, and retelling Genesis.

41. Rabbah bar bar Hana was one of the Amoraim, the scholars whose words about the oral Torah were written down in the Talmud. He lived between 200 and 500 CE for some time in Babylonia and then in the Land of Israel. He's best known for his fantastical sea stories.

42. Rav Huna was a scholar who contributed to the Talmud. He was born in Babylonia (in Tikrit, which you might recognize as the birthplace of Saddam Hussein) in 216 CE and lived there until his death in 297 CE. He was buried in the Land of Israel.

43. Written in Jewish Babylonian Aramaic during the 8th and 9th century in Italy, *Pirqe de Rabbi Eliezer* is composed of stories (*Aggadah*) and interpretations (midrash) of stories from Genesis from creation up until the punishment of Miriam. It includes descriptions of many customs as well as an astronomical section that describes the seven known planets and the signs of the zodiac, and a description of Ezekiel's vision of the Chariot.

44. Bereshit Rabbati was written in the 11th century CE and contains quotes from apocryphal texts, and the use of gematria to interpret Genesis. This text has been cited as proof in Jewish writings that the messiah would have no father, but it does not contain any such quote.

45. Tertullian (155-220 CE) was a Church leader of North Africa who was known for attacking Gnostic Christians. He was the first to use the term "Trinity," but he later had some trouble because his version of the Trinity didn't match what became the dominant view. For this and other similar deviations, he was never designated a saint. He thought that anyone who committed murder, black magic, or sexual sins such as adultery should be kicked out of the Church and not be allowed back in. This fits with how much he attacks the Watchers' teachings. He also believed that widows should not be allowed to remarry, which says something about how he felt about women, although he was himself married. However, he came to believe that marriage was only slightly better than having sex with anyone and that the best marriages did not involve sex at all. He considered that those who abstained from sex, as he did, should hold higher positions in the Church than those who were married and enjoyed sexual relations (the enjoying part he thought specifically should not happen).

46. Cyprian (210-258 CE) was a bishop from Carthage. His early writings were very influenced by Tertullian. He fell out of favor during the Roman persecution of Christians in 250 CE, when he ran away and hid. Many Christians in Carthage signed papers saying they had sacrificed to the Roman gods to avoid persecution. Cyprian railed against them as cowards and demanded that they perform public penance in order to be readmitted to the Church when the persecution ended. These lapsed or "fallen" people often got readmitted to the Church anyhow by getting some celebrity saint or figure to sign a paper saying they had made penance and were true Christians again. This devolved into a schism between different Christian factions in Carthage. Cyprian was beheaded by the Roman government for being an enemy of the gods of Rome. Cyprian is not the same man as Cyprian of Antioch aka Cyprian the Magician, who was a figure of legend rather than actuality.

47. Augustine of Hippo (354-430 CE) was the bishop of Hippo, a city in what is now Algeria. He created the concept of Original Sin.

48. Sheol is a dark, silent place for the souls of the dead in the Hebrew Bible. It's not the same as Hell, but more a kind of waiting area. Souls in Sheol can be raised by necromancers, as the Witch of Endor does.

49. The Testament of Solomon was composed in Greek between the 1st and 13th centuries CE, probably by a Christian writer, but it contains elements of Judaism, Christianity, and Greek religion and magic. It focuses on the story of how King Solomon, who is considered the builder of the First Temple, was helped in this task by demons he compelled thanks to his magic ring.

50. The Diadochi succeeded Alexander the Great upon his death. Their rise coincided with the rise of Hellenism.

51. Not much is known of Athenagoras (133-190 CE) except for his writings. The most well-known was Legatio, which is a defense of Christianity against accusations that it was atheistic (since it rejected the Greek and Roman gods) and involved cannibalism (the Eucharist).

52. Turiel is appealed to for protection in a Jewish Babylonian Aramaic incantation bowl. His name is listed along with other angel names, beginning with Michael and Raphael and some Divine Names.

53. "In Israel" means among the people of Israel, the Israelites, or Jews. They don't have to be living in the Land of Israel or in ancient times. It means basically "among Jews." Even now, a Jewish person gets a name to use "in Israel," which can be anywhere in the world where there are Jews. Nowadays, such names are used only for ritual purposes, like a marriage contract or being called to read the Torah in public.

Bibliography

Bautch, Kelley Coblentz. "What Becomes of the Angels' 'Wives'?" *Journal of Biblical Literature* (Vol. 125, Issue 4) Winter 2006: 766–80.

Bautch, Kelley Coblentz. "Decoration, Destruction and Debauchery: Reflections on 1 Enoch 8." Dead Sea Discoveries, 2008, Vol. 15, No. 1, "Reading between the Lines: Scripture and Community in the Dead Sea Scrolls" (2008), pp. 79-95.

Boccaccini, Gabriele, *Roots of Rabbinic Judaism: An Intellectual History, from Ezekiel to Daniel* (Grand Rapids, MI: Wm. B. Eerdmans Publishing Co., 2001), 249 pp.

Collins, John J. "The Transformation of the Torah in Second Temple Judaism" *Journal for the Study of Judaism in the Persian, Hellenistic, and Roman Period,* 2012, Vol. 43, No. 4/5, *Transformations in Second Temple Judaism: Special Issue in Honour of Florentino García Martínez on the Occasion of his 70th Birthday* (2012), pp. 455-474.

Collins, John J. "How Distinctive was Enochic Judaism?" Meghillot: Studies in the Dead Sea Scrolls, A Festschrift for Devorah Dimant, (Bialik Institute, Jerusalem; 2007), pp. 17-34.

Decock, P. B. "Holy Ones, Sons of God, and the Transcendent Future of the Righteous in 1 Enoch and the New Testament," *Neotestamentica*, 1983, Vol. 17, "Studies in 1 Enoch and the New Testament" (1983), pp. 70-82.

Drawnel, Henryk. "Some Notes on the Aramaic Manuscripts from Qumran and Late Mesopotamian Culture," *Revue de Qumrân*, Décembre 2013, Vol. 26, No. 2 (102), pp. 145-167.

Drawnel, Henryk. "Between Akkadian "ṬUPŠARRŪTU" and Aramaic רפס : Some Notes on the Social Context of the Early Enochic Literature," *Revue de Qumrân*, Mai 2010, Vol. 24, No. 3 (95), pp. 373-403.

Drawnel, Henryk. "The Mesopotamian Background of the Enochic Giants and Evil Spirits." *Dead Sea Discoveries*, 2014, Vol. 21, No. 1 (2014), pp. 14-38.

Duquette, Lon Milo. "Introduction" in *The Book of Enoch the Prophet* (Newburyport, MA: Red Wheel/Weiser, 2012)

Elder, Nicholas A. "Of Porcine and Polluted Spirits: Reading the Gerasene Demoniac (Mark 5:1-20) with the Book of Watchers ('1 Enoch' 1-36)," *The Catholic Biblical Quarterly*, Vol. 78, No. 3 (July 2016), pp. 430-446.

Findell, Martin. "The 'Book of Enoch', the Angelic Alphabet and the 'Real Cabbala' in the Angelic Conferences of John Dee (1527-1608/9)." *Henry Sweet Society Bulletin* (2007) 48:7-22.

Fröhlich, Ida. "The Symbolical Language of the Animal Apocalypse of Enoch (1Enoch 85-90). *Revue de Qumrân*, Avril 1990, Vol. 14, No. 4 (56), *The Texts of Qumran and the History of the Community: Proceedings of the Groningen Congress on the Dead Sea Scrolls* (20-23 August 1989) (Avril 1990), pp. 629-636.

Giulea, Dragoş-Andrei. "The Watchers' Whispers: Athenagoras's 'Legatio' 25,1-3 and the 'Book of the Watchers'," *Vigiliae Christianae*, Aug., 2007, Vol. 61, No. 3, pp. 258-281.

Goff, Matthew. "Gilgamesh the Giant: The Qumran Book of Giants' Appropriation of 'Gilgamesh' Motifs," *Dead Sea Discoveries*, 2009, Vol. 16, No. 2 (2009), pp. 221-253.

Greenfield, Jonas C. and Stone, Michael E. "The Enochic Pentateuch and the Date of the Similitudes." *The Harvard Theological Review*, Jan.-Apr., 1977, Vol. 70, No. 1/2, pp. 51-65.

Greenfield, Jonas C. and Stone, Michael E. "The Books of Enoch and the Traditions of Enoch." Numen, Jun., 1979, Vol. 26, Fasc. 1 (Jun., 1979), pp. 89-103.

Giulea, Dragoş-Andrei. "The Watchers' Whispers: Athenagoras's 'Legatio' 25,1-3 and the 'Book of the Watchers.'" *Vigiliae Christianae*, Aug., 2007, Vol. 61, No. 3 (Aug., 2007), pp. 258-281.

Heger, Paul. "'1 Enoch'—Complementary or Alternative to Mosaic Torah?" *Journal for the Study of Judaism in the Persian, Hellenistic, and Roman Period*, Vol. 41, No. 1 (2010), pp. 29-62.

Huggins, Ronald V. "Noah and the Giants: A Response to John C. Reeves." *Journal of Biblical Literature*, Spring, 1995, Vol. 114, No. 1, pp. 103-110.

Jarosz, Ian. "Homosexuality in Leviticus: A Historical-Literary-Critical Analysis." *James Madison Undergraduate Research Journal*, vol. 9, no. 2, 2022, pp. 33-43. *http://commons.lib.jmu.edu/*

Kam, J. Vander. "The Theophany of Enoch I 3b-7, 9." *Vetus Testamentum*, Apr., 1973, Vol. 23, Fasc. 2, pp. 129-150.

Kiel, Yishai. "Reimagining Enoch in Sasanian Babylonia in Light of Zoroastrian and Manichaean Traditions." *AJS Review*, Vol. 39, No. 2 (November 2015), pp. 407-432.

Knibb, Michael A. "Christian Adoption and Transmission of Jewish Pseudepigrapha: The Case of '1 Enoch.'" *Journal for the Study of Judaism in the Persian, Hellenistic, and Roman Period*, 2001, Vol. 32, No. 4, pp. 396-415.

Kuhn, Harold B. "The Angelology of the Non-Canonical Jewish Apocalypses." *Journal of Biblical Literature*, Sep., 1948, Vol. 67, No. 3, pp. 217-232.

Kvanvig, Helge S. "'Jubilees'—Between Enoch and Moses. A Narrative Reading." *Journal for the Study of Judaism in the Persian, Hellenistic, and Roman Period*, 2004, Vol. 35, No. 3, pp. 243-261.

Lesses, Rebecca. "They Revealed Secrets to Their Wives: The Transmission of Magical Knowledge in 1 Enoch." A draft of a paper, no numbering, no pd.

Martin, Dale Basil. "When Did Angels Become Demons?" *Journal of Biblical Literature*, Winter 2010, Vol. 129, No. 4, pp. 657-677.

Miller II, Robert D. "Shamanism in Early Israel." *Wiener Zeitschrift für die Kunde des Morgenlandes*, 2011, Vol. 101, pp. 309-341.

Newsom, Carol A. "The Development of 1 Enoch 6-19: Cosmology and Judgment." *The Catholic Biblical Quarterly*, July, 1980, Vol. 42, No. 3 pp. 310-329.

Nickelsburg, George W. E., "The Experience of Demons (and Angels) in 1 Enoch, Jubilees, and the Book of Tobit," a paper read at The Philadelphia Seminar on Christian Origins, an Interdisciplinary Humanities Seminar in its twenty-fifth year under the auspices of The University of Pennsylvania, Department of Religious Studies, Philadelphia, PA.

Nickelsburg, George W. E., "Enoch, Levi, and Peter: Recipients of Revelation in Upper Galilee," *Journal of Biblical Literature*, Dec., 1981, Vol. 100, No. 4 (Dec., 1981), pp. 575-600.

Nickelsburg, George W. E., "The Temple According to '1 Enoch,'" *Brigham Young University Studies Quarterly*, 2014, Vol. 53, No. 1, pp. 7-24.

Nickelsburg, George W. E., "Apocalyptic and Myth in 1 Enoch 6-11," *Journal of Biblical Literature*, Sep., 1977, Vol. 96, No. 3, pp. 383-405.

Orlov, Andrei. "Worthless Secrets: Corruption of Cosmological Knowledge in the Enochic Tradition." *Scrinium* (2022), pp. 244-314.

Patai, Raphael. "The God Yahweh-Elohim," *American Anthropologist*, Vol. 75, No. 4 (Aug 1973), pp. 1181-1184.

Peursen, Wido van, "Qumran Origins: Some Remarks on the Enochic/Essence Hypothesis." *Revue de Qumrân*, Décembre 2001, Vol. 20, No. 2 (78), pp. 241-253.

Reed, Annette Yoshiko. *Fallen Angels and the History of Judaism and Christianity: The Reception of Enochic Literature.* New York: Cambridge UP, 2005. 336pp.

Reed, Annette Yoshiko, "Gendering Heavenly Secrets? Women, Angels, and the Problem of Misogyny and 'Magic,'" pp. 108-151 in Kimberly B. Stratton and Dayna S. Kalleres (eds), *Daughters of Hecate: Women and Magic in the Ancient World,* Oxford University Press (Oxford, UK) (2014), 550pp.

Reeves, John C. "Utnapishtim in the Book of Giants?" *Journal of Biblical Literature,* Spring, 1993, Vol. 112, No. 1, pp. 110-115.

Reimer, Andy M., "Rescuing the Fallen Angels: The Case of the Disappearing Angels at Qumran." *Dead Sea Discoveries,* 2000, Vol. 7, No. 3, *Angels and Demons,* pp. 334-353.

Reiner, Erica. "Astral Magic in Babylonia." *Transactions of the American Philosophical Society,* 1995, New Series, Vol. 85, No. 4, pp. i-xiii+1-150.

Schäfer, Peter, "In Heaven as It Is in Hell: The Cosmology of Seder Rabba di-Bereshit," in Ra'anan S. Boustan and Annette Yoshiko Reed, eds., *Heavenly Realms and Earthly Realities in Late Antique Religions* (Cambridge: Cambridge University Press, 2004), 233-274.

Schiffman, Lawrence H. "Pseudepigrapha in the Pseudepigrapha: Mythical Books in Second Temple Literature." *Revue de Qumrân*, Mars 2004, Vol. 21, No. 3 (83) (Mars 2004), pp. 429-438.

Stone, Michael E. "Enoch, Aramaic Levi and Sectarian Origins," *Journal for the Study of Judaism in the Persian, Hellenistic, and Roman Period,* December 1988, Vol. 19, No. 2 (December 1988), pp. 159-170.

Stone, Michael E. "Enoch and The Fall of the Angels: Teaching and Status." *Dead Sea Discoveries,* 2015, Vol. 22, No. 3, "Religious Experience and the Dead Sea Scrolls," pp. 342-357.

Stone, Michael E. "The Book of Enoch and Judaism in the Third Century B.C.E." *The Catholic Biblical Quarterly,* October, 1978, Vol. 40, No. 4, pp. 479-492.

Stuckenbruck, Loren T. "The 'Angels' and 'Giants' of *Genesis* 6:1-4 in Second and Third Century BCE Jewish Interpretation: Reflections on the Posture of Early

Apocalyptic Traditions." *Dead Sea Discoveries*, 2000, Vol. 7, No. 3, "Angels and Demons," pp. 354-377.

Swartz, Michael D. "The Dead Sea Scrolls and Later Jewish Magic and Mysticism." *Dead Sea Discoveries*, Vol. 8, No. 2, "Qumran and Rabbinic Judaism" (2001), pp. 182-193.

Swartz, Michael D. "'Like the Ministering Angels': Ritual and Purity in Early Jewish Mysticism and Magic." *AJS Review*, 1994, Vol. 19, No. 2, pp. 135-167.

Syfox, Chontel. "Israel's First Physician and Apothecary: Noah and the Origins of Medicine in the Book of Jubilees." *Journal for the Study of the Pseudepigrapha* Vol 28.1 (2018): 3-23.

Thom, J.C. "Aspects of the Form, Meaning and Function of the Book of the Watchers." *Neotestamentica*, 1983, Vol. 17, "Studies in 1 Enoch and the New Testament," pp. 40-48.

Thomas, Samuel I. "'Riddled' with Guilt: The Mysteries of Transgression, the Sealed Vision, and the Art of Interpretation in 4Q300 and Related Texts." *Dead Sea Discoveries*, 2008, Vol. 15, No. 1, "Reading between the Lines: Scripture and Community in the Dead Sea Scrolls" (2008), pp. 155-171.

Townsend, Colby. "Revisiting Joseph Smith and the Availability of The Book of Enoch." *Dialogue: A Journal of Mormon Thought*, 2020, Vol. 53, No. 3, 41-72.

Weitzman, Steven. "Why Did the Qumran Community Write in Hebrew?" *Journal of the American Oriental Society*, Jan.-Mar., 1999, Vol. 119, No. 1, pp. 35-45.

Werline, Rodney A. "Ritual, Order and the Construction of an Audience in '1 Enoch 1-36'." *Dead Sea Discoveries*, 2015, Vol. 22, No. 3, "Religious Experience and the Dead Sea Scrolls," pp. 325-341.

Werrett, Ian. "The Evolution of Purity at Qumran," pp. 493-518. In Christian Frevel and Christophe Nihan, eds., *Purity and the Forming of Religious Traditions in the Ancient Mediterranean World and Ancient Judaism* (Leiden, NL: Brill, 2012), 601 pp.

Wright, Archie T. "Some Observations of Philo's 'De Gigantibus' and Evil Spirits in Second Temple Judaism." *Journal for the Study of Judaism in the Persian, Hellenistic, and Roman Period*, 2005, Vol. 36, No. 4, pp. 471-488.

About the Author

Harold Roth is an author and artist and among the foremost authorities on plants within the modern occult community. He has studied Hebrew as well as Jewish mysticism and magic for decades. The author of *The Magic of the Sword of Moses* and *The Witching Herbs*, Harold teaches classes on botanical magic, Kabbalah, and witchcraft. Visit him at *haroldroth.com*.

To Our Readers

Weiser Books, an imprint of Red Wheel/Weiser, publishes books across the entire spectrum of occult, esoteric, speculative, and New Age subjects. Our mission is to publish quality books that will make a difference in people's lives without advocating any one particular path or field of study. We value the integrity, originality, and depth of knowledge of our authors.

Our readers are our most important resource, and we appreciate your input, suggestions, and ideas about what you would like to see published.

Visit our website at *www.redwheelweiser.com*, where you can learn about our upcoming books and free downloads, and also find links to sign up for our newsletter and exclusive offers.

You can also contact us at *info@rwwbooks.com* or at
Red Wheel/Weiser, LLC
65 Parker Street, Suite 7
Newburyport, MA 01950